BUSES

YEAR BOOK

Cover captions:

Top left:
Mayne is the oldest-established of an increasing number of independent operators serving central Manchester. This Roe-bodied Daimler Fleetline is one of five purchased in 1976. It is seen entering Piccadilly in 1987.

Top right:
Badgerline has expanded considerably since becoming an independent company. Among the traditional vehicles in its fleet is this Leyland National 2 inherited from the Bristol Omnibus Co and operating in Bath in 1987.

Bottom left:
Clydeside Scottish was the first major operator to show interest in running ex-London Routemasters and has been the biggest buyer of the type. Most are running in the Paisley and Glasgow areas. Former RM641 is seen in Glasgow city centre.

Bottom right:
Eastern Coach Works developed a double-deck coach body for use by NBC subsidiaries running London commuter services. Most were on long-wheelbase Leyland Olympian chassis but the last four were based on standard 9.5m-long Olympians and were delivered to Alder Valley North towards the end of 1986, shortly before it was renamed the Berks Bucks Bus Co. *Cover photographs by Stewart J. Brown*

£7.00

This page:
An Olympian materialises in the fog on its way to South Croydon. *John Aldridge*

1989

BUSES YEAR BOOK

Edited by
Stewart J. Brown

LONDON

IAN ALLAN LTD

First published 1988

ISBN 0 7110 1785 9

Published by Ian Allan Ltd, Shepperton, Surrey; and printed by Ian Allan Printing Ltd at their works at Coombelands in Runnymede, England

Contents

Below:
The classic Regent III, with equally classic Weymann bodywork which on this Leeds example has unusually deep windows giving it more than a passing resemblance to contemporary Roe products.
M. Dryhurst

Blunderbus

The bus industry has suffered a disproportionately high share of failed designs, argues **Alan Millar**, *as he examines what went wrong — and why.*

It was the poet E. C. Bentley who wrote, *George the Third ought never to have occurred, One can only wonder at so grotesque a blunder,* and turning from poetry to the mundane prose one can only wonder at such grotesque blunders as have been perpetrated in the name of progress in the British bus and coach industry over the past 35 years. There have been some classic examples of sound, efficient, automotive engineering over that same period, but, out of all proportion to the overall experience of road vehicle design elsewhere, there have been some real blunders; whoppers; blinding fiascos which went wrong, if not from Day One, certainly by teatime on Day Two.

Mention names like Wulfrunian, Roadliner, Swift, Panther, Panther Cub, Falcon V — the names go on — and strong men weep, tear out their hair and thump their desks. But why should there have been such a catalogue of disasters? Why, when the failures in the car world are insignificant by comparison with the size of the UK market (it grew from 134,000 vehicles in 1950 to 1.88 million in 1986), should so many designs have given trouble in a market which shrank to 2,100 vehicles in 1986? Before answering these questions, let me allow you to consider some of the facts.

The bus of 1950 differed little from its predecessor of 20 years earlier. It was more powerful, had a diesel engine, possibly some form of semi-automatic gearbox, had better brakes and a more soundly constructed body. But, if it was a double-decker, it still almost certainly had an open entrance/exit at the back, carried around 56 passengers in comfort comparable with the mass market cars of the day and maybe even sported a heater. A single-decker probably had seats for 35 people and a forward entrance/exit.

Left:
Perfection discarded? A classic bus of the early 1950s, a Leyland-bodied PD2 of the South Notts fleet, is followed into Nottingham by a Northern Counties-bodied Lowlander of the same fleet. *Alan Millar*

Above:
Albion's lightweight offerings included the rear-engined Viking which seated only 40 people thanks to engine intrusion at the rear. Most were bought by the Scottish Bus Group; this is an Alexander (Midland) specimen. *Stewart J. Brown*

Progress, developing ideas first tried just before the outbreak of World War 2, was coming in the shape of underfloor-engined single-deckers which, at the expense of poorer passenger access, offered seats for up to 44 passengers.

But the 1950s were when the bubble burst. Petrol rationing ended and, as disposable incomes rose, ordinary people discovered just how inferior the bus was to their own, instantly accessible, private transport. Taking seven buses to reach the countryside, waiting 15 minutes on a wet street corner and having to walk to your final destination might have seemed acceptable before, but not any more and patronage started falling steadily.

Oddly enough, about the only feature of the business which was still about right was the bus itself, but it, probably more than the service it provided, was the target for change in a business which needed imaginative commercial thinking to mould its services to suit changing needs. While market researchers were a species as rare as the dodo in the bus industry at the time, engineers were left the task of creating solutions which, hindsight tells us, did more to prolong and exacerbate the problems than they did to reverse the tide of decline and it was because of this that the industry charged up a blind alley in hot pursuit of a god called Weight Saving. The theory was that if buses were made lighter, they would cost less to build and would consume less fuel. The cost savings reaped would then be a sure-fire way of helping preserve services which might otherwise disappear. What the theorists did not appreciate early enough was that the same lighter buses would be driven nearer to the limits of their endurance, that their lighter components would fail sooner, and that the labour force needed to keep these buses mobile would command ever higher wages which would represent an increasing proportion of the operating costs. So, while first generation underfloor-engined single-deckers like the 7-ton-plus Leyland Royal Tiger and AEC's equivalent Regal IV did nothing to further the cause of fuel economy but in many cases (like London Transport's 25-year-plus, one-million-mile-plus RF-class Regal IVs) lasted years, their lightweight successors were soon displaying weaknesses which would eventually be rectified by making succeeding generations of buses heavier again.

Leyland's 5½-ton Tiger Cub of 1952 and AEC's Reliance and chassisless Monocoach soon gave way to a heavier Reliance and Leyland's Leopard of 1959. The Monocoach and its Leyland equivalent, the Olympian,

Above:
This photograph depicts the first of 60 Metropolitans for the Merseyside PTE. Most were sold off prematurely. *Alan Millar collection*

disappeared fast and such lightweight Albion horrors as the 35-seat Nimbus (341 built between 1954 and 1960), the ultra-light 41-seat Aberdonian (471 built from 1957-60) and the rear-engined Viking (239 built from 1965-70, mostly for the Scottish Bus Group) soon earned reputations which were less than flattering. Bristol, which had built over 300 extremely basic SC4LKs and around 160 Nimbus-related SUs between 1955 and 1966, celebrated its return to the open market with its LH of 1968, a late entrant to the market which, despite substantial sales to National Bus Company fleets and London Transport, was still a lightweight with all the attendant horrors which that entailed.

After weight, height. There was a genuine problem affecting many double-deckers used in areas with low railway bridges. They were too high to fit under the bridges, unless they were fitted with 'lowbridge' bodies which condemned passengers on the upper deck to sit in rows of four reached from a narrow, sunken offside gangway which also intruded into a quarter of the lower deck passengers' headroom.

Bristol, restricted by statute from supplying customers outside the public sector, cracked the problem with the Lodekka, its main series production bus from 1953. By diverting the propeller shaft and fitting a low centre rear axle the seating layout of a higher double-decker was preserved and the technical specification was kept within the bounds of experience. But the companies of the BET group at the time, the major independent companies and the municipals could not buy it and the Scottish Bus Group did not want to depend solely upon it, so the seeds were sown for a mass scramble to build open market equivalents with varying degrees of complexity.

Dennis managed to short-cut the procedures by obtaining licensing rights to build the Lodekka for the open market, badged as the Loline, but Dennis had disappeared from many operators' lists of potential suppliers long before production began in 1957 and only 279 were built over the next 10 years.

AEC, rather than developing its Regent V into a lowheight, created the integral Bridgemaster along Lodekka lines in 1956 and after a production run of 179 developed it in 1962 into the Renown, a separate chassis version of simpler design which achieved 251 sales over the next five years against a falling demand for front-engined buses. Leyland's Atlantean of 1956 developed from a low-height into a full-height double-decker and Daimler's Fleetline of 1960 — like the Atlantean a rear-engined design — was a lowheight from the start which went on to sell to markets hitherto untapped by Daimler and achieved a production run close to 12,000 over the following 20 years.

From the foregoing we can deduce that the Bridgemaster, despite its common engineering with the legendary London Transport Routemaster, was a blunder. Its transmission design led to an awkward amount of intrusion on forward entrance models and the lack of a semi-automatic gearbox ruled out possible sales to many larger municipal fleets. It was bought mainly by those BET companies which were not attracted to the competition.

Leyland fared little better when it met the Scottish Bus Group's demand for a lowheight version of the best-selling Titan PD3. It got Albion to do the job, on the cheap one can only surmise, for when it emerged in 1961 as the Lowlander, it matched a low chassis frame and dropped centre rear axle to a front end nearly as high as on the PD3. The resulting combination could look odd, to say the least, and condemned the two passengers sitting over the driver's cab to higher seats than those in the rest of the bus. Worse still there were reliability problems with them from the start which led two of its bigger customers — Central and Western SMT — to offload examples on to less prosperous SBG companies as soon as was decently possible. Total production over five years was 273, of which SBG took 193.

All of that is but nothing compared with the greatest lowheight fiasco of them all, the Guy Wulfrunian, the biggest flop since Gilford failed to win a single order for its front-wheel-drive trend breaker of 1931.

The Wulfrunian ought to have been a roaring success. Guy still had residual support from the war years when it supplied around 2,500 utility Arabs to bus-starved British operators; and in 1959, while Leyland and Daimler were working on their rear-engined marvels, Guy's new model, with the entrance ahead of the front axle and the engine positioned between the driver and the door, appeared to be closer to what bus engineers were used to.

But while Leyland and Daimler used conventional braking systems and suspension on their otherwise radically different Atlantean and Fleetline models, Guy threw all caution to the wind by using air suspension (independent at the front to improve cornering), disc brakes (lighter and theoretically easier to replace than drums) operated by air-hydraulics, and, to save critical front platform space, used the Cave-Browne-Cave combined saloon heating/engine cooling system with two radiators mounted at the front of the upper deck. The bulky front suspension system intruded to such an extent that the potential payload advantage of not having an engine in the seating area was lost, and the driver was crammed into a smaller cab space than on any other double-decker on the market. In addition, Guy had paid too much attention to the needs of too small a customer, the independently-owned West Riding Automobile Co, which bought new 126 of the 137 built over six years and ended up with six of the others. The combination of so many innovative features deterred the rest of the market, and West Riding soon found a growing list of faults: suspension and steering problems shortened tyre life, electrical weaknesses caused fires, metal fatigue attacked the chassis frames and front hubs and the bodywork was extremely expensive to overhaul. No sooner had West Riding been nationalised in 1968 than the new owners

instigated a scrapping programme which replaced Wulfrunians with secondhand Lodekkas and, later, new Fleetlines with Gardner engines salvaged from the Guys.

Nor had the Wulfrunian saved Guy in its hour of need. The company had fouled up an attack on the South African market in the late 1950s and the new bus was being sold below cost in a desperate attempt to win orders. Guy owed Lloyds Bank £1.3 million in 1961 when it appointed a receiver who sold the company to Jaguar for a mere £800,000. Jaguar already owned Daimler and the combination of the sales forces for the two marques in April 1962 ensured that the better developed Fleetline would succeed. Apart from one order from Guy's home municipality, Wolverhampton, all Jaguar-era orders for the Wulfrunian came from West Riding and it cancelled the last 25 on order.

By then fashion was changing again. Construction and Use regulations changed in 1961 to permit 36ft (11m) single-deckers, and a growing interest in the one-man-operation of buses was leading British operators to ape Continental and American practice and oblige more passengers to stand. The latest response to declining demand was to offer a slower service in less comfort — and with buses which had to be designed from scratch.

Nobody built suitable standee single-deckers in 1961. The Reliance and Leopard were long enough, but their mid engines made the floors too high for urban services, so a whole new range of competing designs of rear-engined, low-framed chassis were launched in rapid succession.

Bristol, ironically, once again got it right from the start. Its RE, with Gardner and (later) Leyland engines, first appeared in 1962, became available on the open market three years later, and enjoyed a production run well in excess of 2,000 vehicles, with over 600 bought new by Ulsterbus and Citybus in Northern Ireland. Nothing else quite matched it.

Daimler suffered from a touch of the Wulfrunians after it unveiled what eventually became the Roadliner. A 1962 prototype with a Daimler engine matured, for want of a happier description, two years later into the production 'real thing' with a completely unfamiliar Cummins V6 engine and air suspension. The engine proved to be as unreliable as it was unfamiliar and later opportunities to buy the bus with a Perkins V8 or short-lived Leyland V8 only creaked production up to 333 vehicles, including coaches and export orders. Only 134 were built for home market bus use, 58 of which were for PMT, the biggest of three customers prepared to place repeat orders. Most were scrapped prematurely.

When Leyland and AEC entered the fray in 1964, their common ownership manifested itself in a common chassis frame design, with provision for a stepped floor rather than the ramped one on the Bristol and Daimler. Leyland fitted largely Leopard running units to create the Panther; Tiger Cub influence went into the smaller Panther Cub. AEC units, drawing on Reliance engineering, created the Swift, except for London Transport whose 11m examples were called Merlins. Panthers were also built in small numbers as coaches and a Leyland V8-engined AEC coach, the Sabre, reached bodied prototype stage in 1970 before being abandoned.

They arrived on the scene as the standee

Far left:
A decaying Greater Glasgow PTE Panther serves as an auctioneer's platform while redundant buses are being offered for sale. It was not even being sold, but had given only about seven years' service.
Alan Millar collection

Left:
A not-so-mobile shop was the unhappy role of an ex-PMT Roadliner with Plaxton bodywork when photographed at a Kent service area in 1978.
Alan Millar collection

Tomorrow never really came for the B15, Leyland's advanced design Titan which became a Concorde of the roads. The first to enter service did so in 1976 with London Transport. *Leyland*

single-decker looked as if it might just oust the double-decker from Britain's towns and cities. One-man-operated double-deckers were not legalised until 1966 and the modern image of the single-decker, exemplified by Sunderland's American-style Panthers, Swifts, Roadliners and REs bought in 1966-68, was taking hold as the industry looked desperately for ways of containing the crisis which was overtaking it.

Leeds bought 150 (mostly Swifts, but also some single-deck Fleetlines), Liverpool 135 (Panthers and REs), Sunderland 90 (mainly Panthers), Manchester 50 (30 Panthers and 20 Panther Cubs) and Birmingham 36 (24 Fleetlines and 12 Swifts). Many other towns and cities bought small batches and London Transport ensured that the Swift/Merlin outsold the Panther by a factor of more than three to one on the home bus market by taking 665 Merlins and 838 Swifts between 1966 and 1971 as part of its Bus Reshaping Plan to operate more short suburban services with one-man buses.

Nobody was really happy with these buses. Passengers often resented having to stand and engineers found that the problems of operating and maintaining them had been underestimated. Overheating problems were commonplace and many bodybuilders failed to build enough strength into bodies which had to support substantial weights on the rear overhang and which in many cases were weakened by having an exit door cut into the middle of the structure. Added to that, the 11m buses were often as much as 3m longer than the buses they replaced; they occupied more space in garages and were difficult to manoeuvre in some suburban streets. It was because of this that London Transport switched to shorter Swifts for the second phase of its purchases.

London's problems exemplified the experiences throughout the country. It was so sick of its purchases that it began large-scale withdrawals in 1973 and was prepared to pay to have them stored on a Hertfordshire airfield while it sought buyers to take them off its hands. By then many other Swifts and Panthers were being sold prematurely by their owners.

British Leyland, which acquired most of Britain's bus manufacturing capacity in 1968, was well aware of the weaknesses of its single-deckers and by 1970 had unveiled prototypes of the mass-produced integral Leyland National, production of which reached a record 7,000-plus over the next 14 years despite early misgivings about the fixed-head 500 engine used in those built prior to 1979. The only all-British competitor to arise from outside, Seddon's Pennine RU of 1969 (a Gardner-engined pseudo RE), ran to a build of 273 buses between 1970 and 1974, but its weaknesses appear to have been every bit as great as those of the older models. BL killed off the Roadliner and Panther Cub first, then the Panther in 1972, the Swift in 1975, but the RE lived on for Ulster until 1982.

As if the foregoing was not enough, the industry went off single-deckers as soon as it discovered them and, before the National was in production in 1972, operators were buying all the double-deckers the manufacturers could supply. Their ability to buy was fuelled by the Government's new bus grant scheme, intended to help the industry invest in one-man buses between 1968 and 1980, but which in many cases was squandered by operators which saw the grant as a way of replacing buses without needing to overhaul them in mid life.

The trouble was that the three double-deck builders all belonged to BL. If you did not want an Atlantean or a Fleetline, there was the Bristol VRT, but it never seemed to recover from its transformation into a transverse-mounted engine layout from its prototypical state with an offside longitudinal engine. It was most popular with National Bus Company fleets which had an obligation then to support a company in which it still had a 50% stake.

Leyland had a project for a new double-decker, the integral B15, on its drawing board with features which operators like London Transport felt a double-decker had to have like hydraulic brakes, independent air suspension and an advanced cooling system. Shades of the Wulfrunian? But as new buses became as rare as gold dust and weaknesses in the designs of the established ranges became ever more apparent, other manufacturers hurriedly developed new double-deckers just like the standee single-deckers had been developed 10 years before.

Ailsa Bus, the Volvo importer, developed a front-engined double-decker with all the qualities that the Wulfrunian could have had, without the drawbacks, but it somehow failed to convince the marketplace in 1973 that it was a serious contender, rather than a place to buy if Leyland could not deliver. Metro-Cammell Weymann, which had developed its Metro-Scania single-decker around Swedish Scania rear-engined running units, launched the Scania-powered Metropolitan at the same time as the Ailsa, won orders for over 600 (including London Transport), but serious corrosion and gearbox problems curtailed its success and many were scrapped prematurely.

Northern Counties, the Wigan bodybuilder, joined forces with Foden, the then independent Cheshire lorry builder, to develop a Gardner-powered rear-engined double-decker, prototypes of which appeared in 1977. Eight were built, seven were bodied and the project died. Dennis re-entered the bus market at the same time, first with the rear-engined Dominator which slowly built up a following, but some other Dennis attempts to please customers too much seemed to blow up in its face. Most notable was a batch of 10 Falcon V coaches built in 1982 for the National Express Rapide services; the mechanical specification, which included a turbocharged Perkins V8 engine, bore too much resemblance to the Roadliner for it to be a success. Falcon V double-deckers, with squat underfloor-rear Mercedes V8 engines, sold only in penny numbers and a demonstrator suffered the ignominy of early retirement to the role of a playbus.

While all of this was happening, Leyland was suffering the combined traumas of effective bankruptcy and its attempts to build and sell the ever more expensive B15. It lurched from being scheduled for building at the National factory at Workington to London Transport's Aldenham works to AEC's Southall factory before it was decided that it would be called the Titan and built at Park Royal's bodyworks in West London. London Transport, which was on the point of a premature scrapping of its Fleetlines, was the main customer, but other major operators had placed orders too. Production began at last in 1978, but stopped early in 1980 after industrial relations problems had so delayed completion of the buses that the Park Royal factory was closed after 250 buses were built for London, 15 for Greater Manchester, five for West Midlands, two for Reading and one for Hong Kong. All other customers were persuaded to cancel their orders and London was compelled to switch its business to Leyland's arch rival, MCW, which had launched its British engineered Metrobus in a fraction of the time Leyland had taken with the Titan and without the troubles experienced with its Metropolitan.

Titan production nearly switched to Eastern Coach Works in Lowestoft, but instead was moved to Workington which turned out 875 vehicles for London, 10 for Reading and one demonstrator before London eventually was prevailed upon to buy the simpler Olympian which had been conceived originally as a lowheight alternative to the Titan but which outlasted it in the end. Titan production ended in 1984. The bus was a white elephant, a Concorde of the roads, overspecified for the job it needed to do, expensive to build, expensive to buy and hardly the cheapest bus to run.

Those, perhaps, are the biggest blunders. One could go on at length about the two-stroke Commers which could not climb hills, the Quest 80 coaches built for Excelsior of Bournemouth which were sold at the earliest opportunity, the Bedford JJL midi-

Below:
One of NBC's Duple-bodied Dennis Falcon V coaches leaving Buckingham Palace conveying the Sri Lanka cricket team. All the coaches were soon sold. *NBC*

bus which impressed nearly everyone who saw it but was never able to buy it, or the ECW coach bodies built for NBC companies in 1982 but which suffered from early structural problems. The list could go on.

London Transport alone is worthy of a chapter on recent bus blunders. The scale of mistakes justifies it, from the purchase and disposal of nearly 1,500 AEC Swifts and Merlins and 164 Metropolitans, through 2,646 Fleetlines to which it took a violent dislike after starving the rest of the country of supplies while it bought them, then the later realisation that they were not that bad and should be kept. LT also spent most of the 1970s trying to develop the XRM, a bus of its own design, then later commissioned Ogle Design to build 'user friendliness' into a future generation of buses which changing operating conditions at the very least postponed for another day. Instead of buying buses with such expensively-researched features as split level steps (already well used in South Yorkshire) and straight staircases (patented in Leeds in the 1930s), London Buses was buying secondhand, notably Ailsas which it shunned for most of their production life, and ironically from West Midlands and South Yorkshire which had bought them in the mid-1970s when Fleetlines were scarce.

And the moral of this tale? Probably that the bus industry ought to have learned the lesson of its first mistakes. It took too narrow a view of how to overcome the problems which started to overtake it in the 1950s and then kept changing the rules every time a new idea had a chance of settling down. Lightweight and lowheight buses did little to enhance the bus service; single-deck citybuses fell from favour before their design was perfected and the next generation of double-deckers was not developed until long after the industry started clamouring for it.

But there is more to it than that. The bus industry is far too small to support the scale of innovation which so many changes demanded. In an age when, increasingly, vehicle manufacturing has become an international affair, with development costs recouped by selling the same products to many different markets, it is asking for trouble to keep making new technological demands on manufacturers before a respectable number of buses can be built. In short, the operators got what they have asked for and got what they deserved.

Fashion has changed again, and minibuses built largely around mass-produced van designs are being used to provide high frequency urban services intended to woo people back on to public transport. The track record of the past 35 years devalues their chances, however, for how can one be certain that this latest sea change in the industry's polices will work any better? But there are some encouraging trends: the buses are cheap to build, easy to maintain and are manufactured in huge quantities as vans. The service is geared more to public demand and there is nothing technically untried about the vehicles.

Time will tell whether we can sit back and reflect with relief that the last of the blunderbuses has gone. Or will the spirit of E. C. Bentley live on?

Below:
Bedford's JJL was widely admired but never entered series production. Most of the prototypes found their way to Brighton Borough Transport.
Stewart J. Brown

A Look at Lincolnshire

Kevin Lane *illustrates the many facets of the changing operations of the Lincolnshire Road Car Company in its final years of NBC ownership.*

Below:
Giving holidaymakers a chance to experience the bracing air of Skegness is this former Southdown Bristol FS6G with convertible open top ECW body. New in 1962, it is seen in Skegness in the summer of 1981.

Top right:
A trio of Bristols on layover in the former Grantham bus station in 1982. Two ECW-bodied RELL6G buses stand alongside an FS5G Lodekka in use as a driver trainer.

Centre right:
In 1981 Lincolnshire was still running this 1966 Alexander-bodied Leyland Atlantean PDR1/1 which it had acquired from Northern General two years earlier. It is seen on the seafront at Skegness.

Bottom right:
This Bristol SC4LK was still in the company's fleet in 1981, although by that time it had been relegated to serving as a mobile office in somewhat incongruous all-over white National livery. It was new in 1957.

LINCOLNSHIRE

EMBASSY
SKEGNESS 596
HJR 656D

NATIONAL

NATIONAL EXPRESS
LINCOLNSHIRE
PRIVATE

SCUNTHORPE
LINCOLNSHIRE
Leyland
C419 VDO

RIBY SQUARE 45
LINCOLNSHIRE
SJA 363J

Left:
The Plaxton-bodied Leyland Leopard seen here was purchased from United in 1980 and was photographed in Dunstable on a private hire trip in 1983. The Bristol RELL about to pass it belonged to United Counties.

Centre left:
A Plaxton-bodied Leyland Tiger in Lincolnshire Coaches livery at Scunthorpe in August 1986.

Bottom left:
If the Tiger/Plaxton represented the cream of the coach fleet, this Leopard/Alexander illustrates the other extreme. It too was photographed in August 1986 and it is seen outside Grimsby depot which has since been closed. The Leopard was later converted to a breakdown tender.

Below:
An ECW-bodied Leyland Olympian in coach livery reverses out of the stand in Scunthorpe bus station at the start of its journey to Hull via the Humber Bridge in 1986.

Bottom:
One of the oldest buses in the fleet in 1986 was this flat-screen Bristol VRT, photographed in Cleethorpes.

602 NEWARK

BCB BASSETLAW
To hire this specially equipped bus
Bassetlaw Community Bus
Bassetlaw Community Bus - your local bus
BRH 181T
LEYLAND NATIONAL
ABBEY NATIONAL
first choice
BACK TO SCHOOL WITH FIRST CHOICE

Facing page, top:
A Bristol LH6L with ECW body passes through Foston on its way from Grantham to Newark in August 1986. This route was truncated with the advent of deregulation to run only from Grantham to Long Bennington.

Facing page, bottom:
This view shows an ex-East Yorkshire B-series Leyland National converted to carry passengers in wheelchairs — note the extra doors ahead of the rear wheel. It is in Bassetlaw Community Bus livery with East Notts fleetnames and was photographed in Retford in 1986.

Above:
During 1986 the company abandoned the Lincolnshire fleetname and chose instead to trade as Road Car, as shown on this ex-East Yorkshire Bristol VRT in Lincoln bus station in 1987.

Left:
Minibuses have been introduced using the fleetname Road Runner. This is a Mercedes L608D in service in the city of Lincoln in 1987.

Scots Minis

Minibuses first appeared in Scottish Bus Group service in 1986 and operations expanded rapidly in 1987. **Ian Train** *illustrates a cross-section of SBG's smallest buses.*

Above:
The first Fife minibus services were started in Glenrothes where this Dodge 'Buzz Bus' was photographed in the summer of 1987.

Right:
The most common type of SBG minibus is the Dodge with Alexander body. Clydeside operate the type in Paisley under the Skipper banner. This one is unusual in having an electronic destination display.

Left:
Eastern started operating a high-frequency minibus service in Edinburgh in October 1986 and expanded its operations in the city in 1987. This is one of the company's original short-wheelbase Dodges.

Below left:
Later Dodges had a longer wheelbase and can be identified by the short window ahead of the emergency door, as can be seen on this Western example, one of 40 introduced on Ayr town services in 1987.

Below:
Deregulation brought competition to the border town of Berwick, notably between Lowland Scottish and Northumbria Motor Services. This is one of Lowland's Berwick Beaver services passing under the town wall.

Top:
Minibus variety appears in the Midland fleet. Midland was one of the first operators to receive MCW Metrorider minibuses. Three were purchased for services in the Alloa area.

Above right and right:
Van conversions have played a very small part in SBG's minibus operations. Kelvin bought Mercedes 608Ds which were converted by Alexander for use on services in Glasgow. The services were not entirely successful and some of Kelvin's minis found their way to other operators including Midland which bought two for use in Linlithgow.

John Aldridge

The Longest Hill

London Transport's route 190 ends at the top of a steep Surrey hill. **John Aldridge** *looks back at some of the variety of vehicles to have climbed to Old Coulsdon.*

It was dark. It was winter. I was a stranger in the locality. It seemed to be the longest hill in the world. The bus, a London Transport RT, had begun the climb in top gear, then third. We stopped at a request stop. A restart in bottom, keep in bottom a while, then change up to second. Not a success, so back to bottom. Eventually the gradient eased and the road swung left. 'This is where we get off', she said, and as we started to make our way downstairs the bus swung right at a crossroads, stopping just round the corner.

Many weekends later, the impression of climbing skywards was confirmed. A notice above the bar at the local pub, the Tudor Rose at Old Coulsdon, read: 'You are now drinking at a height of 537ft above sea level'. The Tudor Rose was, and is, the terminus of the LT 190 bus route. In the late 1950s it was worked, like hundreds of other London routes, by RTs.

More recently it has been through the usual London classes of bus: Routemasters, then conductor-operated (as LT put it), Fleetlines, then one-person-operated Fleetlines, followed by silent encapsulated Fleetlines, and now a mixture of silent Fleetlines and Olympians.

In between, however, it has had more than its fair share of aberrations and added interest. These anomalies include a strange interlude with hired Southend Corporation Leyland Titans and, more recently Metrobuses.

I have omitted one important point. It is mother-in-law's bus route, and such people judge buses and bus routes in a totally different way. Special liveries, or the presence of one of the few remaining top-numberbox RTs, go unnoticed. But a change in garage allocation for the route, from Thornton Heath to Croydon, was quickly and unwittingly spotted. 'The crews aren't so friendly now', she observed one day. Thornton Heath (code TH) was a smaller depot, once a tram depot, and 190 was partly a tram-replacement route. Croydon (TC) was originally one of three Thomas Tilling garages (TC stood for Tilling Croydon) and was a much larger, more impersonal place.

Old Coulsdon had, like much of the area, developed considerably in the 1930s. As the developers edged further out of London and south of Croydon they built mainly along the valleys — the Brighton Road and the

Above:
Almost there! An RT nears the top of the hill on its climb up to Old Coulsdon.

Above:
The descent was easier — a well-loaded RT sets off for Thornton Heath.

Godstone Road, for example. Later they tackled the hills, the easier ones first and then higher and higher. The hill to Old Coulsdon on the 190 route is probably not much steeper than 1 in 10, but it is a long hill and fairly straight. In snow the buses often prudently turn round at the bottom of the hill, though the London Borough of Croydon is far better than many of its neighbours and grits its roads early.

Old Coulsdon is also served by London Country South West (as it now is) *en route* from Croydon the indirect way to Godstone and maybe Reigate (and even Dormandsland on school journeys). Their older-established route (started by the old East Surrey Traction Co) branches off the Brighton Road earlier than the 190 and has an easier though longer climb. Then, a few miles later, it goes down a much steeper incline, Caterham Hill, on which crash gearbox vehicles were used by LT Country Buses for many years.

Back to the 190. Its present form came about as part of the replacement of the Croydon trams. There were two main routes, 16 and 18, which went from Purley all the way to London, round the Embankment, and back — the route number varied according to whether Blackfriars Bridge or Westminster Bridge was crossed first. The other Croydon route was a local service, 42, which ran from Croydon along the 16 and 18 to Thornton Heath Pond and then turned off to the right in an easterly direction to Thornton Heath proper, traversing some interlaced track along narrower parts of Brigstock Road on that last section. The 190 replaced it, but was extended south from Croydon to Purley replacing 166A between Thornton Heath Pond and Old Coulsdon.

Old Coulsdon had first been served by red buses just before the outbreak of World War 2, when route 59B was introduced. It was shaped like a frying pan (the route, not the buses) running up to Old Coulsdon by the country bus route and back by what is now the 190, or vice versa, but with no outer terminal. Special fares enabled people to ride either way round the loop at no extra charge, even if the distance was greater.

A number of Croydon area routes went over to one-man-operation when LT began its big buying spree of first generation rear-engined single-deckers. When they were not a success, one-man Fleetlines generally took over. A flatter route, the 166, which parallels the 190 from Croydon southwards to Purley and then turns off in the other direction to Chipstead Valley, was thus converted, but the 190 escaped.

There is a strange habit, once very common in Manchester and London, of having different routes on Sundays. So on Sundays, Chipstead Valley had a through service to London, the 59, which was a long-established

Above:
The 190 was chosen for the operation of Titans hired-in from Southend Corporation. This is a 1965 PD3 with manual gearbox.

service. When 166 went over to one-man-operation the 59 was diverted on Sundays to replace the 190, and in 1977 that gave Old Coulsdon a sight of one of the Silver Jubilee Routemasters.

Much more colourful, however, was the period when LT was in deep trouble with spares and vehicle shortages in addition to many other problems. That led to a big scheme to hire in buses and coaches from all sorts of operators, but the LT maintenance staff did not like it. So in the end there were only three such schemes; two were routes on which coaches were used, and the third was the 190. It received some very smart blue and cream Southend Corporation Leyland Titans. They were hired for the princely sum of £15 a day each (£90 a week as they did not work on Sundays), with Southend doing the maintenance on them and changing over vehicles when necessary.

The Titans had old-fashioned (by London standards) manual gearboxes so they were obviously unsuitable for central London work. Something quieter and more 'outer suburban' was what was needed, but the trouble was that almost all such routes had already been converted to one-man-operation, and an open rear platform is of no use. Thus the 190 was chosen, though one could hardly call it a quiet route. And of course the drivers on the 190 rota all had to do type-training on the Titan and learn to master a part crash, part synchromesh gearbox.

I made a number of end-to-end trips on the Titans — what enthusiast living locally would not? Usually they were toward the end of the evening rush hour. Not infrequently we stopped at every single stop, as well as numerous traffic lights, pedestrian crossings and traffic blockages in between. One evening one driver crashed every single gear. Most drove them well, though one told me he finished every shift with an aching left foot and left shoulder (they did not have power steering, either). But even the best drivers, if they stopped at that request stop part way up the hill to Old Coulsdon, had to stay in bottom gear until the very top.

In due course — too soon for me and too long for the crews — the Titans vanished to start new lives with London Country at Harlow, and the Routemasters returned to the 190.

Routemasters actually returned for a surprisingly long time, time enough for the gold RM (RM 1983, of course) celebrating LT's 50th anniversary (1933-83) to appear on the route. By now we were also into the showbus era and Croydon garage favoured RM1000 for this. This vehicle gradually appeared to go backwards in time as various bits and pieces, once standard on earlier RMs reappeared.

That was a good year for the 190. Croydon centenary year was celebrated by a Fleetline painted in the old Croydon Corporation tram colours, with the figure 100 writ large on the front panel and, sometimes, an appropriate wording in the front intermediate destination box, and that bus too appeared on the 190 from time to time.

The appearance of this Fleetline and others was an indication of the forthcoming replacement of the Routemasters. Initially, there was a fairly motley collection of Leyland/Daimler Fleetlines but later Croydon became a stronghold of the encapsulated engine Fleetlines. They make a sound all of their own, and one which reminds me of wartime sirens sounding.

I doubt that many passers-by notice the difference — even mother-in-law has never commented. The result is perhaps a demonstration of the results of do-gooders meddling in the bus industry, for the quiet Fleetline was a whim of the former Greater London Council. Gardner declined to be involved in the project, taking the view that its engines were not noisy, or should not be tampered with anyway. So they are all Leyland-engined and, yes, they may be a bit quieter. But, subjectively, the traditional noise of a Fleetline is merely suppressed, to be replaced by other noises from the transmission and auxiliaries which previously one could not hear.

Once LT started disposing of the Fleetlines it seemed likely that all would go, but rumour had it that Ensign, which bought most of the others, was not convinced that operators would be too keen to buy quiet Fleetlines and so these 400 have remained with LT. Quite recently I overheard an LT engineer admit that, properly maintained, the engineering cost of a Fleetline was a penny a mile or so below that of a Metrobus.

Because the quiet Fleetlines were expected to be disposed of they had enjoyed little in the way of scheduled repaints or overhauls, but

Far left:
Conductor-operated Daimler Fleetlines have shared operation of the 190 with Routemasters, one of which can be seen in the background of this view at the Old Coulsdon terminus.

Left and below left:
Among special Routemasters to have served on the 190 are the gold-liveried RM1983, commemorating 50 years of London Transport, and Croydon garage showbus RM1000, with an appropriate advertisement on the side.

Bottom:
The Croydon Centenary DMS ran on the 190. Here it passes through Purley on the main Brighton to London road.

more recently there was a scheme to start this work. To help create a float, a dozen or more Metrobuses were drafted into Croydon though in the event the overhaul plan was dropped. Currently, however, not only a lick of paint but also a major gearbox improvement is being applied to them.

Croydon's Metrobuses were fairly regular performers on the 190 among other routes, but they vanished in 1987 — to be replaced by a much larger number of brand new Leyland Olympians. The Olympians have been joined by the three 1984 Olympians that were part of LT's big experiment — Alternative Vehicle Evaluation, they called it — to compare them with Metrobuses, Volvos and Dennises.

So these days, and even on Sundays, the next 190 might be a B20 Fleetline, or one or other of the Olympian types.

On weekdays, there is a rival route too. For during LT's troubled period, if I may so call it, there were many complaints about the 190. That led LT to let London Country divert some of the buses on its older established 409/411, via the 190 and my hill. They are numbered 411 and produce the occasional green Leyland National (if things are desperate), but mainly Park Royal or Roe-bodied Atlantean AN68s, Olympians, or even ex-Greater Manchester Atlanteans.

In bus spotting terms, mother-in-law has never had it so good.

Right:
More recently Metrobuses and Olympians have appeared. A Metrobus picks up passengers as it leaves Old Coulsdon.

Below:
Even Surrey gets snow. Quiet B20 Fleetlines have been regular performers alongside the more recent Olympians.

Distractions

Mark Alexander *surveys changing fashions and the buses which went with them.*

Left:
In the late 1950s and early 1960s long-haired ladies liked to pile their hair on top, increasing their apparent height considerably. This had two advantages for the colleen conductress standing here beside the time clock. Firstly, the style prevented curtains of hair obscuring her view of the Ultimate ticket machine and her coin bag. Secondly, it cleaned the bus ceiling — Birmingham City Transport, whose bus this is, was noted for its tidy bus fleet. Both the hairstyle and the bus, a 1948 Daimler CVG6 with Metro-Cammell body, were rather out of date by the time this view was taken in February 1968.

Below:
Miniskirts are associated with the 'Swinging Sixties' but probably reached their shortest in the early 1970s. Having reached the point of no return, hemlines plunged in 1973-74. The driver of the West Midlands PTE Marshall-bodied Daimler Fleetline seen here survives this distraction in October 1972.

Left:
Gary Glitter is widely credited with encouraging the platform shoe fad of the mid-seventies. However, as all bus enthusiasts know, the real reason was the arrival of high-floor underfloor-engined stock on to Birmingham city services after part of Midland Red was taken over by West Midlands PTE. The girl on the right in platform shoes has a one step advantage over the other passengers preparing to mountaineer into this BMMO S17 in July 1976.

Below:
The mid-1970s saw one of the periodic emergences of tight sweaters. The white belt, however, is a distinctive feature of the period combined, no doubt, with flared trousers. This severely attractive young lady has alighted in September 1977 from one of the last halfcabs in the Birmingham area, a 1963 Midland Red BMMO D9.

Above:
Leather has regularly featured in ladies' wardrobes ever since the exquisite Honor Blackman as *Avengers girl* Cathy Gale, first caused male toes to curl in the early 1960s. The decadent aspect of its image was adopted enthusiastically but scruffily by the punk movement in the late 1970s. Punk was briefly cleaned up and borrowed by the mainstream fashion market as 'punk chic' — our model outside the Canolfan Gwaith (otherwise known as the Jobcentre) seems to be the only person in view not getting on or off this Cardiff Alexander-bodied Bristol VRT in April 1982. Black and white does no justice to the hair colour.

Below:
Youth fashion in the 1980s has split into several camps, each coming unhealthily pre-packaged with its own clothes, hairstyles, music and even political and racial viewpoints. For example, someone favouring sharp suits, a skinhead haircut, country music and the Liberal/SDP Alliance will find themselves falling between several cult packages. The black leather jacket remains a useful bridge between sub-cultures, however, and the formidable young lady advancing on this Midland Red South Leyland Olympian/ECW at Stratford-upon-Avon in May 1984 could pass for punk, greaser, heavy metal fan or Pansy Potter.

Top:
The ebb tide of the punk era has left a legacy of scruffy dress and attitudes. Can these Saturday outfits be expected to attract the opposite sex? Also looking scruffy is this ex-Oxford Daimler Fleetline/ Northern Counties double-decker, of Green Bus, at Cannock bus station. Its appearance is unusual for the operator, but forgiveable, since country roads in December are not conducive to clean buses.

Above:
Currently short hair is almost compulsory for the fashionable female, often with more than a hint of men's styles of the late 1950s. Little Richard would recognise the hairstyle of this young lady passing a London Buses MCW Metroliner loading in Colmore Row, Birmingham, in May 1986.

Amazingly Excellent Chassis

AEC's long-lived Regent double-deck chassis was launched in 1929. AEC enthusiast **Michael Dryhurst** *pays tribute to the model on its 60th anniversary.*

Rather like Coke and Pepsi in the soft drinks business, the main rivals within the British passenger vehicle building industry were Leyland Motors Ltd and the Associated Equipment Co Ltd, better known by the initials AEC.

In 1923 AEC had introduced its NS-type double-decker, the first to boast a cranked chassis profile to give a lower rear platform with a consequent improvement in boarding for the passenger. This concept, and the execution thereof, was updated considerably in 1927 when Leyland brought the Titan TD1 on to the market. This vehicle was acknowledged as the contemporary ultimate in double-deck design, the appeal of the chassis

Left:
This particularly fine preserved Regent III captures all that was 'amazingly excellent' about the model. It was operated by York Pullman and had bodywork built in Yorkshire by Charles H. Roe of Leeds. Like AEC, neither York Pullman nor Charles H. Roe are still with us.
Stewart J. Brown

Top:
London General was an early devotee of the Regent with the first examples forming the ST class. This is ST264 in original condition at Holborn Circus.
London Transport

Right:
The most famous Regent of all? This is the prototype of London's RT class - RT1.
London Transport

Above:
Roe rivals. Two preserved Roe-bodied buses of the 1930s at London's Covent Garden. On the left is a Regent from the Leeds Corporation fleet and on the right is the rival Leyland Titan, from Lincoln.
M. Dryhurst

being enhanced considerably by the Leyland-built lowheight body which featured a sunken gangway on the offside of the upper deck to permit a lower overall height and much operational advantage. It also brought the word 'lowbridge' into the bus vernacular. The vehicle was an immediate success.

AEC, although at that time a subsidiary of the Underground group of companies (and thus an associate of the London General Omnibus Co whence came the company title), was not confined to the Underground group in its sales and enjoyed considerable sales both in provincial Britain and abroad. The company had enjoyed a brief association with the Daimler company (Associated Daimler), but by the end of the 1920s had gone its own way including the move from Walthamstow to the famous site at Southall, Middlesex. In 1929, AEC introduced three new passenger chassis — the single-deck Regal, the three-axled double-deck Renown and arguably its most famous chassis, the double-deck Regent. These three were all-new designs with a new range of AEC petrol engines and a number of other contemporary design features.

All three models were well received, the Renown particularly so by London General which operated the buses as its LT class, subsequently using a single-deck version as well, plus three experimental double-deckers of its own construction but modelled closely on the Renown. Equally, the Regal had enormous instant appeal and soon found its way into many company fleets particularly as a coach. But undeniably the flagship of the new range, indeed for AEC itself, was the Regent. Naturally, General ordered the model in large numbers for which it became the famous ST class and the model soon became a familiar sight far and wide, with operators such as Birmingham, Cardiff, Devon General, City of Oxford, Halifax, Thomas Tilling, Eastern National, Newcastle, Glasgow — the list is too long!

As built originally, the Regent was 25ft long, with a wheelbase of 15ft 6½in and was fitted with an AEC six-cylinder 6.1-litre petrol engine, the type receiving model designation 661. Brakes were mechanically operated by a single servo but were updated in 1932 with vacuum-hydraulic operation, whilst in the previous year the wheelbase had been extended to 16ft 3in (hence the LGOC STL class, with 'L' indicating 'long'). Also in 1931 a compression-ignition oil engine had been introduced, of 8.8 litres capacity, a

Right:
Ipswich Corporation's first motorbuses were Regent IIIs, delivered in 1950, and from then until 1966 all of the undertaking's new double-deckers were Regents. This picture shows a 1955 Regent III with 61-seat Park Royal body passing Electric House as it arrives at the town centre in January 1974. *Stewart J. Brown*

Below:
Portugal was a major export market for Regent IIIs and Regent Vs. A 1951 Weymann-bodied Regent III with a vaguely appropriate Anglophile destination bounces over Lisbon's indifferent road surfaces in 1979.
Stewart J. Brown

Left:
Glasgow Corporation specified a non-standard new-look front for its Regent Vs. In 1961-62 a batch of 89 buses was delivered for tramway replacement. They were 30ft long 72-seaters with Alexander bodywork, and were the last of a long line of AECs to be purchased by Glasgow. The city's first Regents arrived in 1930. *Stewart J. Brown*

Below:
Southampton Corporation bought Regent Vs between 1961 and 1967. The first 10 had uncompromisingly upright Park Royal bodywork.
Stewart J. Brown

7.7-litre version being made available in 1932, during which year the Wilson pre-selector gearbox with fluid transmission was offered as an option. In 1933 the famous Gardner engine range became available in the Regent in both 5LW and 6LW versions, and as the oil engine was now the principal power source the model became designated 0661.

During the 1930s the specification was revised continually, culminating in 1939 with that most famous of British double-deckers, the RT. World War 2 caused AEC vehicle production to be curtailed, although in 1942 a number of chassis were completed from prewar components. Regent production resumed in 1945 with a somewhat austere basic 7.7-litre crash gearbox model known as the Regent II (but still coded 0661), this being replaced in 1947 by the classic Regent III. At the same time the RT-type Regent III was also being built — 4,674 for London Transport, 40 for St Helens and one for Coventry Corporation, along with 60 earlier provincial RTs. In 1949 the company built the Regent IV which was a revolutionary underfloor-engined double-decker but which did not go into volume production, and the last-of-the-line Regent V appeared in 1954 as a 27ft-long chassis, being available shortly thereafter for 30ft-long bodywork. The merger with Leyland in 1962, but more importantly the 1968 Bus Grant scheme, saw the end of the AEC Regent in 1969.

Above:
The Regent III enjoyed considerable success in overseas markets including Australia, South Africa and the Iberian peninsula where this bus is seen working in Lisbon. It has Weymann bodywork.
M. Dryhurst

Right:
The last big overseas order came from the Kowloon Motor Bus Co and called for 34ft Mark V models capable of carrying 120 passengers. This one had MetSec/KMB bodywork.
M. Dryhurst

Buses Past My Door

Stewart J. Brown *reviews the buses which have served him in the varied places in which he has lived.*

Titles are often difficult. My first try was 'Buses at the bottom of my garden' — a sort of pun on the old saying about fairies, but it is neither a good pun nor a very accurate one. Indeed, to describe my interest in gardening as minimal is to verge on gross exaggeration. I am an avid anti-gardener and where possible have tried to live in a house *sans jardin*, as the French might say. So it is 'Buses past my door'; a quick reminisce.

The first door I can remember living behind was up a close in Glasgow, which may be the deep-seated root of my aversion to gardening. As they say in Glasgow's Chinese quarter: 'He who lives up close has no garden'. Very profound. This close may also just have something to do with my interest in buses. Why? Because to my great delight one day in 1954 Glasgow Corporation started to put up wiring for a trolleybus terminus right outside my house. I cannot pretend that at the tender age of six I had any great interest in buses, but as soon as erection of the wiring commenced I cherished the fond hope that trolleybuses were going to be running through Glasgow with 'Inglefield Street' writ large on the destination blind. My street was going to be famous. But, alas, Inglefield Street was not to achieve immortality (until now, at any rate) because the terminus was named Govanhill. Perfectly appropriate I must admit — but a bit vague. After all, to a six-year-old Govanhill was, if not the centre of the universe, a Very Big Place.

Below:
Services through Govanhill were provided by Glasgow Corporation. An Alexander-bodied Daimler CVD6 pauses in typical surroundings.

105
say— McVITIE'S the word before Biscuits
TCHIE
322
RPLUS STORES
FYS 796

38
ROUKEN GLEN
SCHREIBER now make kitchen units
59
MOSSPARK
D220
SGD 203
SGD 152
GRANT

Top left:
A Glasgow Corporation BUT trolleybus passes within a stone's throw of the Govanhill terminus. A total of 90 BUT 9613Ts, with handsome Crossley bodywork, joined the Glasgow fleet in 1957-58. Trolleybus operation ceased in 1967. *Stewart J. Brown*

Bottom left:
Modern Daimlers formed the mainstay of services on the south side of Glasgow in the early 1960s. Both these buses are Alexander-bodied CVG6s; the leading vehicle dates from 1959 while the following one was new in 1957. They are in the simplified livery adopted in 1959 to facilitate spray painting. *Stewart J. Brown*

Above:
Leyland Tiger Cubs delivered to Alexanders in the late 1950s were originally allocated to long-distance services but later found their way on to local routes. This 1971 view shows a 1959 Tiger Cub in Falkirk bus station in Alexander (Midland) bus livery; when new these dual-purpose vehicles were painted predominantly cream. *Stewart J. Brown*

Glasgow's trolleybuses, incidentally, gave me my first — and last — introduction to Latin. The intermediate destination blind contained a list of places served which was headed by the word 'via' — not a word heard on the lips of Glaswegians every day and one which had to be explained to me.

Let me move on a few years — barren years of busless interest and a fear of school teachers — to the next door. This was in Castlemilk, a few miles further south from the centre of Glasgow and the largest municipal housing scheme in Europe. (In Glasgow there was a subtle linguistic differentiation between private houses which were built in 'estates' and council houses which were built in 'schemes'.) Size may be a dubious claim to fame, but large areas of high-density housing needed frequent bus services and Castlemilk was generously served. None passed my door in the way the occasional Govanhill-bound trolleybuses had, but there were five frequent routes within a few minutes' walk.

The Corporation's Leyland Titan PD2/24s were much in evidence (there were, after all, 300 of the beasts) but a high proportion of the Castlemilk services were provided by the infinitely preferable Daimler CVG6s. These had pleasantly-proportioned Alexander bodies and throaty Gardner 6LW engines. The rounded lines of the Birmingham-style new-look front of the earlier machines matched the curves of the Alexander body. Nice buses. They were the cream of the Castlemilk fleet in the early 1960s, but older buses abounded.

Castlemilk sits atop a hill and two routes were operated largely by Albion Venturers which made their way up with a melodious gearbox whine. AEC Regent IIIs (occasionally) and oldish Daimler CVD6s (frequently) also toiled their way to Castlemilk. A selection of long-forgotten (or do I mean best forgotten?) body-builders' products were fitted to these early postwar buses — Scottish Aviation, Northern Coach Builders, Croft, Brockhouse, Roberts. There was no standardisation there.

Castlemilk, like most places on the tops of hills, lacked a railway. But genteel Kings Park, a 1930s suburb a mile or so nearer the city centre, was served by the new British Railways Glasgow suburban electric service — the 'Blue Trains'. Transport planners in big cities (or major conurbations, to use the jargon) had this idea that it made sense to carry large numbers of people by bus to railway stations and tranship them on to trains. Beyond certain distances this is not an unreasonable idea. Castlemilk was not beyond that certain distance, however, as the short-lived 'Blue Train Bus' — a service operated by forward-entrance AEC Regent Vs — proved.

I travelled on its last evening of operation. The tickets which were issued on the bus on journeys to the city were collected by BR ticket collectors at Central station and I wanted some examples for my collection. I was the only passenger on the bus (a fairly typical load). 'Two and two halves to Central station, please', I asked. The conductor looked at me. Then he looked for my non-existent fellow travellers. 'Pardon?' he asked. Glasgow bus conductors always were polite, even to suspected lunatics.

My next stop was London - Kennington Park Road, near the tube station. Here the London Transport 109 ran from house door to office door, a distance of about 1½ miles. However, traffic congestion around the Elephant & Castle was so bad in 1968 that it was almost as quick to walk. So I rarely sampled the delights of travel on London Transport's RTs, preferring to walk or to take the tube. This was, of course, in pre-DMS days, but rear-engined buses ran past my office door to Waterloo: XA-class Atlanteans and the unique rear-engined Routemaster, FRM1, while the first of the production batches of AEC Merlins were entering service on the expanding Red Arrow network.

Overall, London's buses were distinctly old-fashioned. I had left a city where half of the bus fleet had forward or front entrances to come to one where virtually every bus was of open platform layout. The RT and RM may have been classics, but London's bus design had stood still in the 1960s.

My next move was north to Aberdeen. In winter. With snow. And ice. Aberdeen gets very cold in winter. Here my local buses, passing within about 50 yards of my door, were provided by Aberdeen Corporation. One route was served by Fleetlines and Atlanteans which were still crew-operated at this time, and the other was worked by one-man-operated AEC Swifts. Like all modern Aberdeen buses they had Alexander bodywork.

In the morning peak one of the few Daimler CVG6s which had been converted from open rear platform to forward entrance would often roll up. These were used as OMO buses but had one major problem: if a passenger failed to pay his fare and did not hear (or heed) the driver's shouts then the unfortunate driver had to get out of his cab, walk

Right:
Castlemilk was generously served by high-frequency routes. A Leyland Titan PD2 waits with a Daimler CVG6 at Castlemilk terminus. Both have 61-seat Alexander bodies.

Facing page, top:
In London it was almost as quick to walk to work as to take a bus. An RT and Routemasters have little traffic to contend with, however, in this view taken near the Elephant & Castle on a gloomy morning in 1969.

Facing page, bottom:
Aberdeen Corporation's fleet included dual-door AEC Swifts, bodied by Alexander. The weather was at times severe.

CAR HIRE
Lock up London
12
ELMERS END GARAGE
NO DEPOSIT
LLU 732

15
MAYFAIR
HAIR FASHIONS
TEL. 556.

round the front of the bus, and hunt down the errant passenger who would invariably be sitting near the back of the upper saloon. Aberdonians throw money about like a man with no arms, and I did see drivers having to abandon their cabs more than once to enforce the payment of fares.

Next stop Falkirk, where I contrived to live in Stewart Road and work in Brown Street (I kid you not!), travelling the distance between these points in whatever might happen along. This was usually a Leopard running on a trunk service to Glasgow or a Fleetline on one of the Falkirk area local routes, both fairly typical Alexander (Midland) buses. However, Leyland Tiger Cubs were preferred to either of these types. Most of the Tiger Cubs had Albion five-speed constant-mesh gearboxes and though Glasgow Corporation's Albion Venturers had long since gone to the great bus garage in the sky, their spirits lingered on in Tiger Cub gearboxes.

Compared with Aberdeen, Falkirk was warm, but neither could compare with my next door which was located in Kisugu, a few miles from downtown Kampala, then seat of power of one Idi Amin, esq. Kisugu lay on Uganda Transport's hourly service from Kampala bus station to Gaba, a route some five miles long. This only needed one bus. Occasionally a Fiat 643E would appear, but more commonly — and appropriately for me — Glasgow-built Clydesdales were used.

Below:
The oldest buses in operation in the South Croydon area in 1972 were RTs in both London Transport and London Country service. A London Country example, new in 1954, heads for Sanderstead and points beyond. *Stewart J. Brown*

Right:
The newest London Country buses included a batch of 11 Daimler Fleetline CRL6s, with Northern Counties bodies, delivered in 1972. They had originally been intended for Western Welsh. This one is seen near London Transport's South Croydon depot. *Stewart J. Brown*

Bottom right:
London Transport's unique rear-engined Routemaster was put out to graze on the 234 service. It is seen here on a bleak January day in 1973 picking up passengers for Selsdon. *Stewart J. Brown*

BARGAINS
GREEN LINE
GREEN ROVER
Purley Old Coulsdon
Caterham Godstone
411
REIGATE
LONDON COUNTRY
JPK 105K
TOP KNOT
BUS STOP

GREEK
WINES & SPIRITS
the immortals
Dick EMERY
ASTORIA
234
Wallington
Woodcote Green
Foxley Lane Purley
SELSDON
OOh.. you are awful
METROPOLE
LONDON TRANSPORT
FRM1
PAY AS YOU ENTER
Exact fare please
KGY 4D

Right:
London Country was one of the local operators in Sanderstead and used Routemasters, RTs, and the then new Swift single-deckers. This is a Routemaster near Sanderstead station.

Below:
Falkirk provided such civilised buses as this Alexander-bodied Leyland Tiger Cub in the Alexander (Midland) fleet. The short bay amidships housed the emergency exit and was a characteristic feature of Alexander bodies of the late 1950s.

These had locally-made standee bodywork. Passengers paid the conductor as they boarded by the rear door; the exit was at the front. The Clydesdales had Leyland 400 engines and semi-automatic Pneumocyclic gearboxes. In Scotland I had thought that the 400 engine was not exactly over-powerful in a 41-seat Tiger Cub — I was speechless when I counted 120 passengers alighting from a Clydesdale.

This was a period of long distances between consecutive doors. As Idi Amin awarded himself the VC, proclaimed himself King of Scotland and exterminated his opponents, Kampala became, metaphorically speaking, too hot for comfort.

Sanderstead in leafy Surrey provided my next door and brought me back into contact with London Transport's route 109 again, at this stage nearing its suburban extremity at Purley, and still RT-operated in 1974. It also renewed my acquaintance with FRM1 and the XA class, now operating from nearby South Croydon garage, and introduced me to the RF-class of AEC Regal IVs which operated on one local route.

Here my nearest public transport was, dare I say it, provided by Southern Region trains on a line which did actually run along the bottom of my garden. The buses which actually passed nearest to my front door were provided by London Country — a mixture of RTs, Routemasters and Swifts in a variety of liveries as London Country switched from dark green and yellow to corporate National Bus Company leaf green and white. After

Facing page, top:
Despite the Leyland badging this is a Gardner-engined Guy Victory operated by Rustenburg Bus Services. The 65-seat body is by Bus Bodies of Port Elizabeth.

Facing page, bottom:
The highlight of the East London fleet was a trio of RTs, all with forward entrances and rear staircases.

DUKA
WINKEL
123

E. L. M. T.
60
CE-18728
BRADLOWS
VIR FOR
MEUBELS FURNITURE

PRUDENTIAL
REYNOLDS FA
COLCHESTER
20
TOWN & COUNTRY
8071 ML

2A
MAGDALEN WOOD
71
TPU 71R

overloaded Ugandan Clydesdales they seem a bit tame.

Eventually a change was deemed desirable. Rustenburg, centre of platinum mining, provided my next abode. Rustenburg, in South Africa's Transvaal province, was hot: literally. The Kalahari Desert was not really close — but it was not really distant either. Protea Park in suburban Rustenburg was served by, surprise, surprise, Rustenburg Bus Services. RBS ran only two types of buses: Fiats and Guy Victorys, both with vertical front engines. The Fiats were nondescript. No, I have nothing against foreign buses, even Italian ones, but given the freedom to express an opinion I would say the Italians' real forte is restaurants, not buses.

With the natives of Wolverhampton the reverse is probably true (well, have you ever had a good meal in Wolverhampton or come across Wulfrunian cuisine in Italy?). The Wolverhampton-built Guy Victorys were magnificent. A little basic perhaps, but still magnificent. A bit like latter-day Daimler CVG6s, in fact, with their Gardner engines and semi-automatic gearboxes, and, since the engine was inside the saloon, it was possible to savour the Gardner sound effects to the full. This is perhaps another way of saying that the Victorys were a trifle noisy, but I come to praise Victorys, not to bury them, and the RBS Victorys are definitely all-time favourite buses.

And then to Cambridge. No, not *that* Cambridge . . . in East London . . . no, not *that* east London . . . East London, Cape Province. Here the bus which ran past my door was provided by East London Municipal

Top left:
Colchester hosted numerous interesting independents, foremost amongst which was Osborne of Tollesbury. Osborne's fleet in 1978 included this AEC/Park Royal Renown which had started life in 1962 as a demonstrator in London Transport Country Area green livery. *Stewart J. Brown*

Bottom left:
A brand-new Leyland Atlantean AN68 in Colchester High Street in the spring of 1977. The combination of Atlantean chassis and ECW body was the Colchester Borough Transport standard at this time.
Stewart J. Brown

Below:
Probably the only bus in Britain to have deliberately matching route and registration numbers was PGX 235L of Continental Pioneer. Here it leaves the centre of Richmond for the short run on route 235 to the top of Richmond Hill. It was a Willowbrook-bodied Ford. *Stewart J. Brown*

Top:
Colchester's standard new buses in the late 1970s were ECW-bodied Leyland Atlanteans. This one is seen at the bottom of East Hill.

Above:
Richmond Bridge is the setting for this London Transport Routemaster in the summer of 1979.

Top right:
Ribble provide the bulk of services past doors in rural Lancashire. A Leyland National climbs through Brinscall on its way from Blackburn to Chorley.

Transport. The standard buses on the Cambridge service were Mercedes-Benz O302s, bringing a touch of sophistication to this narrative. But never fear — behind the sophistication lurked a few more familiar buses. AEC Regal IVs ran past my door for the first time (apart from the odd London Transport RF which ran near Sanderstead). Better still, I had my last encounter with RTs which occasionally ventured out to Cambridge, usually appearing at lunchtime on school journeys. And no ordinary RTs either. None of your antiquated open platform buses here, but forward-entrance RTs, running OMO. ELMT ran three such machines in 1976.

But it takes more than a RT, or even three RTs, to tie me down. The next stop was Colchester. No catch this time, Colchester, Essex, which is a bit like Castlemilk — built on a hill. Here, for the first time, my door, on the eastern edge of the town centre, was served by a variety of operators. Least frequent was Eastern Counties, running Bristol FSs, Bristol REs or Leyland Nationals, all displaying the informative destination 'Service'. Residents of Eastern Counties territory in the late 1970s were lucky to find the name of their town on a bus, never mind the name of their street. Then came Eastern National, usually with Bristol MWs or Leyland Nationals. The real local operator was, of course, Colchester Borough Transport. CBT's regular buses on my route were Leyland Atlantean AN68s with ECW bodies and my main impression was one of service reliability, something which it is easier to achieve in a small town than in a large conurbation — sorry, big city.

My next destination was to be Richmond. No, not Richmond, Virginia. Certainly not Richmond, North Yorkshire, but the posh one: Richmond, Surrey. If I am honest, it was the East Twickenham end of Richmond. Or even the Richmond end of East Twickenham. Either way, it was 2min walk from Richmond Bridge which was traversed by a fine selection of London Transport buses and Routemasters, Bristol LHs, Leyland Nationals and brand new Metrobuses all made their way back and forth across the Thames. If I cared to walk 5min into central Richmond I could see Continental Pioneer's 235 service to the top of Richmond Hill, usually operated by an RF or by the Willowbrook-bodied Ford bought specially for the service and registered PGX 235L. Dare I stick my neck out and say that it is the only bus ever purchased in Britain with a registration number to match its route number?

So far all has been urban. Even Rustenburg was more or less urban. The next move brought a change: a touch of country life.

Right:
New to the Richmond area in 1979 were London Transport's first MCW Metrobuses. The early deliveries had white upper deck window surrounds and (shock, horror!) reflective number-plates, as illustrated by this bus in Richmond town centre. *Stewart J. Brown*

Below:
Withnell lies in the rural belt on the western edge of East Lancashire. A Ribble Bristol VRT on the route from Blackburn to Chorley illustrates the point. *Stewart J. Brown*

Far right:
Winter in Withnell. A Ribble Leyland National 2 climbs out from Withnell towards Abbey Village in February 1981 on its way to Blackburn. Prior to deregulation Ribble provided all services around Withnell; now contracted services are in the hands of other operators.
Stewart J. Brown

Cows, sheep, goats, cocks-a-crowing, milk maids-a-milking and even SJB-a-gardening (reluctantly and infrequently). This door was in Withnell Fold. Suddenly even Kampala sounds important. Withnell Fold did not actually have buses other than on daily school contracts but Ribble provided a link with civilisation — if such a term can be applied to Blackburn and Wigan — with an hourly service between these two points which passed Withnell Fold Road End. The service was largely operated by Leyland Nationals with the occasional Bristol RE or VRT.

The most recent move was a short one, two miles to Withnell just before Deregulation in 1986. Before Deregulation my front door in Withnell was busless (although there were buses nearby), but Deregulation actually did bring buses past my door again in the shape of the hourly Ribble service from Blackburn to Wigan, re-routed away from Withnell Fold Road End and directed through Withnell. For some 12 months it was operated jointly with the newly-formed North Western company whose red and blue bus enlivened the scene once every three hours, before the whole service reverted to Ribble. Blackburn Transport run past on schools services and I have an independent too, Reeve's Coach Hire, running shoppers' services to Blackburn and to Chorley using elderly coaches.

The Ribble buses are noticeably less interesting than those which passed my previous doors. No Routemasters. No RTs. Certainly no Guy Victorys or Daimler CVG6s. Not even the odd Albion Venturer. Only Nationals. Sometimes National 2s or VRTs. Maybe sometimes an Olympian or (once) the company's only Lynx. Meanwhile in Castlemilk Magicbus is running Routemasters, buses which I had admired from afar when I lived there in the mid-1960s — maybe I should have stayed in Castlemilk . . .

Martin S. Curtis

Bristol's Last Lightweight

Bristol's LH chassis was the longest-lived of its successive lightweight models. **Martin S. Curtis** *tells the story.*

When the Bristol LH chassis first appeared in 1967 few thought that this would be the last lightweight design to emerge from the Bristol works.

Bristol Commercial Vehicles (and its predecessor, the Bristol Tramways & Carriage Co Ltd) had been building passenger vehicles since 1908 and among the wide range of vehicles produced from that time were a succession of lightweight models. Moreover, Bristol's products (together with those of Eastern Coach Works) had only recently returned to the open market following the Leyland/Transport Holding Co share exchange of 1965. Thus Bristol was able to exhibit its models at the 1966 Commercial Motor Show, after an absence of 18 years.

Bristol was therefore looking optimistically to the future and viewed enthusiastically the prospect of supplying not only established customers from the nationalised sector, but also new buyers who had not been in a position to purchase new Bristols for some years.

At the time of the LH's launch, the longitudinally-engined double-deck VR chassis had recently been introduced, while the very successful RE and FLF Lodekka models

represented the bulk of production. However, a slot for the LH had been created in the Bristol range by the withdrawal of the underfloor-engined MW saloon and lightweight SU models, both of which had ceased production shortly before. With the opportunity to sell its models to both new and traditional customers, Bristol ensured that the LH was designed to be an extremely versatile chassis aimed at capturing a broad section of the market for lightweight buses and coaches.

The first LH (Lightweight chassis, Horizontal engine) was a prototype with chassis number LHX.001 and was of standard, intermediate length. With a wheelbase of 16ft 2in, this version was intended to carry bodywork of some 30ft in length. Power was provided by a Perkins H6/354 six-cylinder, 5.8-litre engine, supported by the chassis behind the front axle, which was linked to a BMC rear axle through a Turner/Clarke five-speed gearbox. Extensive use was therefore made of proprietary units, as had been the case with several previous lightweight Bristol chassis.

A front-mounted radiator was employed to take full advantage of the natural airflow as the vehicle moved forward (this having become the standard position on Bristol chassis) while the fitting of a spring parking brake was verging on the revolutionary and the LH (together with Bristol's soon-to-appear VRT double-deck chassis) would be the first British production passenger chassis to include this feature. Indeed, the cab layout as a whole was very modern and uncluttered by contemporary standards with the cab floor, side and instrument facia produced from glass reinforced plastic mouldings, resulting in a notably draught-proof cab.

With weight distribution in mind, a 25-gallon fuel tank was located on the outside of the main chassis frame ahead of the rear axle on the offside, while attached in the corresponding position on the nearside was a battery cradle. Semi-elliptic springs were fitted as standard on both axles with hydraulic shock absorbers mounted additionally at the front.

Chassis LHX.001 received a 45-seat ECW stage carriage body with a flat front, which strongly resembled that fitted by ECW to RE service buses but with longer bays. Registered NHU 100F and finished in a livery of

Below left:
An LH chassis on delivery from Bristol. Note the front-mounted radiator and the temporary lighting. Most LHs went to Lowestoft to be bodied by Eastern Coach Works. *M. S. Curtis*

Below:
The third prototype LH was fitted with a Weymann body transferred from an Albion Nimbus. It was operated by Western Welsh. *M. S. Curtis*

Tilling green and cream, this vehicle became a Bristol-ECW demonstrator, in which role it remained until sold to Eastern Counties in 1970.

A second LHX prototype followed, powered by a Leyland O.400 6.54-litre engine, which was initially sent to Strachans for bodying. However, this did not come about and instead this chassis received a Plaxton Derwent bus body incorporating 2+3 seating at the rear to achieve a seating capacity of 49. It eventually entered service in 1969 with Golden Miller of Feltham (registed CJJ 44H) which already operated 10 LH coaches by that time.

The third and final prototype was a short (12ft 6in) wheelbase LHS model which entered service with Western Welsh in 1968 again powered by a Leyland O.400 unit and carrying a Weymann 30-seat bus body which had been transferred from a 1961 Albion Nimbus. Western Welsh considered the possibility of transferring further bodies to LHSs but in the event did not do so, leaving LHX.003 (MBO 1F) to remain unique.

Full production commenced in earnest from 1968 and the LH attracted considerable interest from operators — indeed, over 240 orders had been received by the spring of that year. Tilling group operators, who became part of the newly formed National Bus Company from 1969, opted for the LH and, to a lesser degree, the LHS service bus, while many independents favoured the LH for coach duties, including the long (18ft 6in)

Above:
The unusual combination of Bristol LH chassis and Duple Viceroy-style 41-seat bodywork was specified for 12 coaches delivered to the Royal Blue fleet in 1970. This one is seen near London's Victoria coach station during the 1973 August Bank Holiday weekend.
Stewart J. Brown

Above right:
In the 1970s Epsom Coaches ran a mixed fleet of full-size Leyland Leopards and short Bristol LHSs. A Plaxton-bodied LHS passes through Trafalgar Square, London, in 1978. *Stewart J. Brown*

Right:
Early ECW bodies on the LH had flat glass windscreens with the original design being slightly shallower than on this York-West Yorkshire LH6L.
M. S. Curtis

EPSOM COACHES
Epsom Coaches
GNM 232N

204
Good old-fashioned security...
We'll build your future on it.
SCARBOROUGH
BUILDING SOCIETY

450 NORWICH BUS STATION
EASTERN COUNTIES
WEX 929S

Wallace Arnold
HWU 83N
YCV 163J

PASSINGFORD BRIDGE
Chase Cross
Stapleford Abbots 250
KJD 407P

wheelbase LHL chassis which completed the LH range. With a choice of three chassis lengths, bodywork of between 22ft and 36ft could be accommodated on the LH and with the further possibility of body width varying from 7ft 6in to 8ft 2½in the basis for the Bristol LH's wide appeal becomes clear.

The 1968 Commercial Motor Show saw the Bristol LH exhibited for the first time. On Bristol's own stand, alongside a new VRT chassis, was an LH6L carrying a 41-seat Plaxton Panorama Elite coach body in the colours of Golden Miller (VOY 12G). A second Golden Miller Plaxton coach, this time on an LHL chassis (TMT 764F), was also available for inspection in the demonstration park. In addition, a third LH was displayed on ECW's stand in the form of an LH6P for Eastern Counties, LH692 (RAH 692F) with standard 45-seat bus bodywork.

As production became established it was clear that the standard LH was by far the most popular variant. Some chassis received semi-automatic transmission incorporating a Wilson epicyclic gearbox and it was anticipated that fully automatic transmission would become available later. It was also planned to introduce a left-hand drive version of the LH though no LHs were ever actually constructed to this configuration. However, a number of chassis were built in CKD (completely knocked down) form and assembled in the Irish Republic by Ascough, the Dublin dealer, before joining operators in Southern Ireland. In Northern Ireland, where Ulsterbus became famous as a major operator of Bristol RE saloons, over 100 LHs also appeared from 1968 in the Ulsterbus livery of blue and ivory with bodywork built

Above left:
The final style of standard ECW bus body for the LH had double curvature BET windscreens. This 43-seat LH6P was delivered to Eastern Counties in 1978.
M. S. Curtis

Centre left:
The LH found its way into many independent fleets. This Plaxton-bodied LH6L was owned by Wallace Arnold and operated in the company's Devon fleet which had a need for coaches small enough to negotiate narrow winding roads. *M. S. Curtis*

Bottom left:
London Transport bought 95 LH6Ls with semi-automatic gearboxes and 7ft 6in wide ECW bodywork. This example was photographed in Romford in 1976. *M. S. Curtis*

Below:
A small number of LHs were fitted with pantechnicon bodies. This Vanplan-bodied LH was operated by Wilson of Guisley, makers of Silver Cross prams.
Leyland

GRANGE ESTATE
to SAVE THE BUSES
42
PHG 242P
29
28
26

PEDESTRIAN
NEWPORT ROAD
294 STOKESLEY
UNITED
NGR 670P

Above left:
Preston Borough Transport operated a trio of Bristol LHS6Ls with neat 31-seat Duple Dominant bodies. New in 1976, they were for a time the only single-deckers in an otherwise all-Atlantean fleet. *Stewart J. Brown*

Left:
United Auto, serving remote tracts of northeast England, built up a large fleet of LHs. Most were LH6Ls with standard ECW bodywork, as shown here in Middlesbrough bus station. *Stewart J. Brown*

Above:
London Transport's BL-class Bristols were LH6Ls with 39-seat ECW bodies. They were unusual in having Pneumocyclic gearboxes. *Stewart J. Brown*

initially by Potters of Belfast, and later Alexander.

Following the formation of the National Bus Company in 1969, ownership of Bristol Commercial Vehicles was equally shared between NBC and Leyland and, perhaps not surprisingly in view of this, Leyland's engine for the LH — with its distinctive tones and greater popularity than the Perkins unit — eventually became standard.

At the 1970 Commercial Motor Show two LHs were again displayed inside Earl's Court. On Bristol's stand an LH6L chassis was on show which subsequently received an ECW bus body before joining the Western National Omnibus Co. Western National became the single most important customer for the LH and eventually received 267 examples of the LH and LHS types with bus or coach bodywork supplied by Duple, ECW, Marshall and Plaxton.

As with most Bristol chassis, Eastern Coach Works became the principal body-builder for the LH and on its stand at the 1970 Show there was once again exhibited an LH6L bus (XRM 100J), on this occasion in the livery of Cumberland Motor Services and featuring a BET-style curved windscreen.

Significant numbers of Bristol LH chassis became increasingly familiar in the fleets of independent operators, with the vast majority of LHLs joining this sector. All LHLs with PSV bodywork received coach bodies by either Duple or Plaxton, with the exception of the only bus-bodied LHL to be built which was bought by Coity Motors in 1970 (registered ATG 459H) with 55-seat Plaxton Derwent bodywork. Among larger operators to buy substantial numbers of LH vehicles were Eastern Counties, Hants & Dorset, Lincolnshire and United Automobile. In Scotland, Alexander (Midland) and Eastern Scottish became the only Scottish Bus Group

Table 1: Bristol LH bodywork

Bodybuilder	LHX	LH	LHL	LHS	Total
Eastern Coach Works	1	1,063	—	153	1,217
Plaxton	1	183	159	118	461
Potter/Alexander (Belfast)	—	111	—	—	111
Alexander (Falkirk)	—	75	—	—	75
Duple	—	29	4	14	47
Marshall	—	10	—	20	30
Northern Counties	—	20	—	—	20
Willowbrook	—	10	—	—	10
East Lancs	—	—	—	2	2
Wadham Stringer	—	—	—	1	1
Weymann	1	—	—	—	1
Goods bodywork	—	4	11	—	15
Total	3	1,505	174	308	1,990

Table 2: Principal Bristol LH customers

	LH	LHL	LHS	LHX	Total
Bristol	116	—	—	—	116
Crosville	56	—	—	—	56
Cumberland	18	—	—	—	18
East Kent	—	—	4	—	4
East Midland	17	—	—	—	17
Eastern Counties	66	—	5	—	71
Eastern National	4	—	—	—	4
Hants & Dorset/ Wilts & Dorset	129	—	—	—	129
Lincolnshire	100	—	10	—	110
London Country	—	—	67	—	67
Midland General/ Mansfield District	18	—	—	—	18
National Welsh	—	—	9	—	9
Southern Vectis	5	—	11	—	16
Southern/Western National	244	—	23	—	267
Greenslades	12	—	—	—	12
Ribble	—	—	2	—	2
Thames Valley & Aldershot	43	—	—	—	43
Timpson	—	—	1	—	1
Trent	6	—	2	—	8
United Auto	219	—	—	—	219
United Counties	13	—	—	—	13
West Yorkshire	32	—	—	—	32
Western Welsh	—	—	—	1	1
Alexander (Midland)	41	—	—	—	41
Eastern Scottish	34	—	—	—	34
Ulsterbus	110	—	—	—	110
Cardiff	—	—	2	—	2
Greater Manchester PTE	6	—	3	—	9
Greater Glasgow PTE	—	—	1	—	1
Northampton	—	—	2	—	2
Preston	—	—	3	—	3
Rossendale	—	—	2	—	2
Tyne & Wear PTE	—	—	1	—	1
West Yorkshire PTE	—	—	12	—	12
Lancashire United	20	—	—	—	20
London Transport	95	—	17	—	112
Independent operators	97	163	131	1	392
Bristol demonstrator	—	—	—	1	1
Goods vehicles	4	11	—	—	15
Total	1,505	174	308	3	1,990

operators of the type, all of which carried attractive Alexander bodywork.

In 1972, Bristol Omnibus received the first of 116 ECW-bodied LH6Ls when six 43-seat buses with semi-automatic transmission were delivered. Surprisingly, perhaps, these were the first LHs to be added to the Bristol operating fleet.

During the same year LHs were once more on display at the Earl's Court show, although it was significant that as from that year Bristol's stand became more closely integrated with those of the Leyland group. On this occasion an LH6L chassis was on display while ECW followed tradition by displaying an LH6P bus (for Eastern Counties) on its stand, and this example (HAH 537L) was one of the first buses to appear in public carrying NBC's poppy red livery.

A third LH model was also on display at Earl's Court and could be found on the stand of commercial bodybuilder, Marsden. This was not a PSV at all but a pantechnicon on an LH6L chassis, which was the first of 14 LH and LHL types supplied to Wilson & Silver Cross of Guiseley for use in the delivery of prams and baby carriages. In addition, a further goods LH (built in 1972) became a racing car transporter with Duple bodywork, but although the Silver Cross LHs became well known throughout Britain and Europe no further goods LHs were supplied to other customers.

While Bristol vehicles were commonplace in most parts of the country, relatively few had ever entered service in the London area. However, the LH represented an exception to this rule since the first of 67 ECW-bodied LHSs was delivered to London Country Bus Services during 1973, while in 1975/6 London Transport received 17 ultra-short LHSs, followed by no fewer than 95 LHs with 39-seat ECW bodies. The latter were fitted with semi-automatic transmission which, by this time, was not normally offered as an option on the LH.

It was a narrow-bodied 35-seat LHS bus for London Country (GPN 311N) which appeared on ECW's stand at the 1974 Commercial Show while, at the same exhibition, a coach bodied LHS with Plaxton's new Supreme coachwork was included as part of that bodybuilder's display of vehicles.

Although Leyland continued to hold only a 50% interest in Bristol, its influence in the affairs of the works became increasingly apparent. At the 1976 Commercial Show, which would be the last such exhibition at which the LH would appear, a bare LHS

Above:
An unusual combination for an independent operator was Marshall bodywork on the short wheelbase LHS chassis. Harvey of Mousehole bought this example for the service from Mousehole to Penzance which was operated jointly with Western National who used similar buses. *M. S. Curtis*

chassis could be seen as the sole Bristol vehicle in the main Leyland display (although an LHS bus for Trent and a VRT double-decker were exhibited by ECW).

Unfortunately, by the mid-1970s severe restrictions had been placed on the availability of the Bristol RE saloon in an attempt to boost sales of the Leyland National bus, production of which was running far below the capacity of the Workington factory where it was produced. Accordingly, it was decided to introduce a Series B version of the 10.3m Leyland National from 1978 which was a simpler and less expensive version of the basic National design. This was aimed at capturing a significant portion of the Bristol LH market although the nature of the two vehicles was radically different and only NBC orders showed any noticeable swing away from the LH. Nevertheless, with the top end of the LH market catered for by the Series B National, Leyland proposed to offer a truck-derived chassis to replace the lower end of the LH range, leaving the Bristol product apparently doomed to disappear altogether within a short space of time. This prospect received little enthusiasm from many operators and despite the arrival of the front-engined Leyland Cub chassis in 1979 the LHS, in particular, had developed a strong following among independents and even some NBC companies.

Obviously in recognition of the LHS's popularity (and to the detriment of Bristol and Leyland) the uncertain future of the LH prompted the introduction of both Bedford and Ford short wheelbase, mid-engined chassis from 1978, which were to compete directly with the LHS coach, leaving observers to speculate whether the proposed demise of the LH had, in fact, achieved what had been intended!

Production of the standard LH model eventually came to an end in 1980 when Bristol Omnibus received AFB 597V, the last of 1,507 LH chassis to be built. The LHL had also been phased out by this time. The LHS continued a little longer however, owing to its popularity, and Leyland was under some pressure from customers for it to remain available. The list of LHS operators was extremely varied and included British Airways, Epsom Coaches, Gash of Newark,

KNIGHT & CROSS LTD
Building Contractors
HIGH ST.
EARLS BARTON
NORTHAMPTON 810500
9 ROUND SPINNEY
BRISTOL LH
21
KBD 21V

Above left:
Rossendale Transport purchased this ECW-bodied LHS6L from London Country in 1983. It was new in 1977, and joined two LHSs purchased new by Rossendale. *Stewart J. Brown*

Left:
Northampton Transport standardised on Bristol VRT double-deckers in the late 1970s and also bought a pair of ECW-bodied LHS6Ls. They were 30-seaters and entered service in 1979. *Stewart J. Brown*

Above:
Production of Bristol lightweight chassis ended with this LHS which was fitted with Plaxton 33-seat coachwork and delivered to Bere Regis Coaches. Shortly before the demise of the model, Leyland toyed with the idea of marketing the LH as the Leyland Cheetah — but in the end decided against it.
M. S. Curtis

Harvey of Mousehole, National Welsh, Northampton Corporation, Park's of Hamilton, Roman City of Bath, Rossendale Transport and Western National to name a few. However, the final batch of LH-type chassis was assembled from late 1981 to early 1982 when the last LHS chassis rolled off the Bristol production line, together (surprisingly) with two further LHLs, the first to be built for over two years. The latter were the final Bristol vehicles to be received with van bodies by Lawrence Wilson & Son. The last LH of all, however, was an LHS with 33-seat luxury Plaxton coachwork which entered service with Bere Regis & District, registered CLJ 413Y.

Altogether 1,990 Bristol LH range chassis were produced for an extremely wide range of operators, many of whom found that the chassis exactly suited their operating requirements. Despite considerable efforts to withdraw the chassis earlier, customer loyalty, which seemed to be in-built in so many Bristol models, resulted in the LH remaining available for 15 years and no doubt would have led to the development of further lightweight chassis had the Bristol factories not been closed following a total takeover by Leyland in the months following the end of LH production. Its place has now been taken by the Leyland Swift which is the current mid-engined lightweight chassis produced in two lengths by Leyland Bus.

Substantial numbers of Bristol LHs remain in regular operation however (including some sold for further service overseas), which is remarkable in view of the lightweight nature of the chassis. The LH is therefore destined to be familiar in Britain for the remainder of the 1980s and beyond, as a reminder of Bristol's last lightweight.

Crosville in Wales

Crosville's long history of bus operation in North Wales took an interesting turn in 1986 when the company was divided into two separate units in preparation for privatisation. The English company retained the Crosville name while the Welsh operation became Crosville Wales. **Reg Wilson** *looks back at Crosville in Wales over the last 20 years.*

Below:
Holyhead depot in 1986 with Willowbrook-bodied Leopards, Leyland Nationals and a solitary Leyland Olympian. In the foreground a Class 08 diesel shunting locomotive is coupled up to the Irish boat train. This view is from the deck of the ferry *St Columba*.

Top right:
In the mid-1960s Crosville still had a large fleet of half-cab single-deckers. This 1952 Bristol LL6B is typical of the type and was among the last to be bought. It was photographed in the autumn of 1966.

Centre right:
A 1960 Bristol MW6G executes a three-point turn in the village of Corris — the only way it can negotiate the hairpin bend. It has a 41-seat ECW body and is one-man-operated, something that was still comparatively uncommon in 1966 when this photograph was taken.

Bottom right:
The lightweight Bristol SC had been developed for use on rural bus services and Crosville built up a large fleet of the type, most of which had ECW 35-seat bus bodies although there were also a few coaches. The SC had a front-mounted vertical Gardner 4LK engine. This 1960 example is laying over in Cardigan in 1972.

LLANDUDNO
VIA
MAESDU
M10
NFM 35

BRAICH COCH
HOTEL
GIVE
WAY

CARDIGAN
45
THE LAMB INN
Crosville
649 LFM
ADP 188K

Right:
Illustrating the remoteness of parts of Crosville's Welsh territory is Cwm Penmachno, where this 13-year-old Bristol MW6G, devoid of fleetnames, was photographed in 1973. NBC's corporate fleetname was carried above the side windows on single-deck buses so that advertisements could be carried on the lower panels without rendering the bus anonymous.

Centre right:
Ten Leyland-engined Bristol REs with ECW's neat coach bodywork were purchased in 1972. Later in their lives they were repainted in NBC's local coach livery, as shown on this vehicle bound for Pwllheli in 1983.

Bottom right:
In 1980 Crosville was buying secondhand double-deckers from many sister companies in NBC. Most were Bristol VRTs, the company's standard type, but there were also some Daimler Fleetlines which were purchased from Southdown. New in 1970, this CRG6LX had Northern Counties bodywork. Is is seen in 1981 carrying Wrexham fleetnames — many NBC subsidiaries adopted local identities as part of their marketing strategy at this time.

Facing page, top:
A bolder marketing move was the adoption of a bright apple green and white livery for Olympians with coach seats which were used on the Cymru Coastliner service from Caernarfon to Chester. The dragon on the side is red.

Facing page, centre:
The new Crosville Wales company adopted a livery of emerald green and white with a stylish new fleetname. This 1978 Leyland National B-series, photographed in Bangor, was one of the first buses to be repainted.

Facing page, bottom:
Gwynedd Council persuaded local operators to promote a common image by simply painting the fronts of their buses red while leaving the sides and rear in fleet livery. This 1981 Bristol VRT — one of the last to be delivered to Crosville — is in NBC leaf green with a red front and with 'Bws Gwynedd' fleetnames supplementing the company's own name.

CROSVILLE
FISH & C
CAERNARFON · BANGOR · CONWY · LLANDUDNO · COLWYN BAY · RHYL · DEESIDE · CHESTER
COASTLINER
CROSVILLE
Leyland
B204 DTU

N79
CROSVILLE WALES
TOCYNNAU CRWYDRO
£2·10 DYDD
£1·55 SUL
99c NOS
HMA 571T

N88 Caernarfon
BWS GWYNEDD
BWS GWYNEDD
CROSVILLE
N89
DCA 636P
DCA 530X

Geoff Mills

Winning at Wembley?

Major events at Wembley attract buses and coaches from all over Britain, and attract bus and coach watchers too. Veteran bus and coach watcher **Geoff Mills** *looks back over the last decade or so.*

Facing page, top:
This 1958 Bristol SC4LK belonging to Alpine Coaches of Dagenham was pressed into service carrying Arsenal supporters in 1978. The wording in the destination box describes it as a 'vintage' bus, but some would deny it this distinction and just say that it was old. It was originally operated by Lincolnshire Road Car.

Facing page, bottom:
Brentwood Coaches ran this 1966 Bristol FLF6G, with chromed wheel trims, which they purchased from Bristol Omnibus in 1978. It is followed into Wembley by another Bristol — a Plaxton-bodied RE bought new by S & M Coaches of Benfleet.

Above left:
Newly acquired from Western SMT, this 1965 Leyland Leopard was owned by Prospect of Lye when photographed at Wembley in 1980. It was new to North Western and had Alexander Y-type bodywork of a style fitted to most Scottish Leopards.

Left:
By 1981 AEC Regents were few and far between. This 1963 specimen with Roe bodywork had been new to Grimsby-Cleethorpes Transport and had passed to Davian Coaches of Enfield in 1976.

Below:
This 1972 AEC Swift was being used to convey police officers for crowd control duty in 1984. It was owned by Franklin's Coaches of Borehamwood and had been new to Aberdeen Corporation. It has 43-seat Alexander bodywork.

Above:
Another bus which originated north of the border was this long wheelbase Daimler Fleetline, at one time operated by Dundee Corporation. New in 1975, it is seen in 1985 running for the Waltham Cross Bus Company. The two-door Alexander body seated 83 passengers.

Above right:
Jonckheere sold a very small number of coach bodies in Britain in the early 1970s before attacking the market more successfully at the end of the decade. This AEC Reliance with Jonckheere Solaire bodywork dated from 1973 and was originally owned by Whitworth of Ashford in Kent. It was photographed in 1985 in service with Harris of Catshill, a Midlands operator.

Right:
Photographed in 1987, this three-axle Bedford VAL was a late example, entering service with Red Car Hire of Loughton in 1973 and seen with Avon of Romford, its second owner, 14 years later. It had 53-seat Plaxton coachwork.

'You're Interested in What?'

There are times when enthusiasm for transport can be difficult to explain. **Peter Rowlands** *tries.*

Blackburn on a grey spring morning. I face a stationary Leyland Atlantean at point blank range, camera poised. A middle-aged man in a raincoat shambles up and places himself in my line of sight.

'Are you going to take a photograph of that bus?'

I lower the camera and look at him for a moment.

'I thought I would, yes.'

'What for?'

I have to think about this. What for? Well, because I am here and the bus is here, and it is not a chance I get very often. But I am not sure that this would satisfy him. Why, in fact, should I want to photograph a bus at all?

It's a fair question, and one I'm often asked — although not usually, thank goodnes, by people who are preventing me from doing it. Why buses? Why photographs of them? Why articles about them? What is there to say?

It was borne upon me long ago that there is no real answer. People who can not see the interest are seldom persuaded by anything I can tell them, and people who can see it do not need to ask. Yet this knowledge does nothing to halt the enquiries.

The man in the raincoat is waiting for a reply. So I tell him, 'Your buses are really interesting'.

Remarkably, he seems to find something informative in this evasive comment. He nods judiciously and edges out of my vision. So I get my picture just as the driver is preparing to leave.

But would it not be nice, just once in a while, to have some proper answers ready? Compelling answers that might even arouse a modicum of interest, or at least attest to one's general sanity. Is it possible?

Transaction apparently completed, the man sidles off.

Right:
Anti-deregulation publicity provides extra interest in this 1985 view of an East Lancs-bodied Leyland Atlantean from the Blackburn fleet. Its green and cream livery harks back to the era before the red, white and green used on the Atlantean in the background.

'You're interested in what?'

People in bus queues pass the time in a lot of different ways. Some chat. Some read. Some stare. Most keep glancing down the street. The one thing they have in common is that they always manage to identify their bus.

But what do they see? Something large? Something coloured? Something with windows all over it? A sort of blur with doors and seats?

Try asking them. It can be an education. They don't want to seem as if they go round with their eyes shut (although some probably do) but they do not want to admit they are particularly interested either, so most likely they will just keep up the wry amusement at you. They don't take any interest in buses because 'One Doesn't'.

Why doesn't one? After all, one takes an interest in plenty of other unlikely things, but they all have unofficial ratings on an acceptability scale. Hang gliding, for instance, would probably get a 10 (romantic and daring). Sailing, maybe eight or nine. Radio ham, around three (learned but a bit esoteric). But buses? Zero. Too commonplace by far. You might get a better score by saying that you study automotive diesel technology or urban mass transit systems. At least they sound a bit special.

Now if it were trains, you'd be in a different league. Trains have always been celebrated by writers and the media. Being interested in railways has the clear stamp of social approval.

Maybe the people who claim not to notice buses really don't. But then, perhaps they did until the veil of conventionality blocked the view.

'You mean you collect bus numbers?'

No I do not collect bus numbers. Nor have I ever done so. In fact, I seldom even look at bus numbers if it is registration numbers you are talking about.

Probably I should. I am always getting caught out by knowledgeable friends poring over my photographs. 'An ex-Southdown Leyland Atlantean', they will pronounce sagely over a bus in someone else's fleet. It implies some obscure cognitive power. I assent cautiously, hoping they will think I photographed the vehicle for that very reason. Then it occurs to me that they are identifying the bus by its registration number.

Do they memorise the registrations for different areas deliberately, as part of an exercise to extend their knowledge? Or do the characters leap off the number plates at them spontaneously? Or then again, does the habit hark back to distant days spent with notebooks on street corners?

While their eye for such detail dismays me, I have to admit I feel some kinship. Photographing buses has definite parallels. Each picture gives you a sense of possession, a feeling of snatching something of your own from the passing scene. Never mind if you do not always recognise the registration, and have to look it up afterwards. The point is it is yours, it was gained by your own endeavours and, like childhood fleetbooks with a few ticks missing, your collection always lacks the ones that escaped. Time will not stand still. Buses get bought, sold and scrapped. Life turns into perpetual pursuit.

Maybe I do collect bus numbers — in spirit, anyway.

'Why are the buses round here called Dennis?'

Yes, why are they? Well, you could say it is because two people with that surname (John and Raymond, actually) started making buses back in 1904. Or perhaps more pertinently, it could be because the present-day company started making modern buses in 1977 after sticking mostly to dust carts and fire engines for about 10 years.

But I suspect this is not what was meant by the question. It is a challenge, really. It says, 'I've noticed something about buses. So tell me, if you can, something more about them that's as interesting as my interest'.

Could anything be? Parry the thrust. 'Some buses are called Leyland'. Clever. 'Ah, but that's the make. I'm talking about those Dennis nameplates on the front.'

Does anyone with this much grasp actually want to know any more? The trouble is, telling them is irresistible. 'If you're talking about double-deckers, there are four British makes nowadays. Leyland is one and Dennis is another. Metro-Cammell Weymann and Volvo are the other two. Bristol and Daimler are two more makes you might see, but Leyland took both those over, and eventually closed them down.'

'Volvo is Swedish.'

'Yes, but it had a factory in Scotland. And, by the way, Scania sells double-deckers here too. They really are made in Sweden.'

'So it's easy to tell a Dennis from a Leyland, is it?'

'Actually no. Often they look almost identical. That's because these companies only make the chassis. Almost everything

Above:
Pale window rubbers on this Park Royal-bodied Leyland Atlantean of London Country give a hint of its origin with Southdown (London Country's were always darker). Otherwise, to the cognoscenti at least, the registration number might have provided the best clue. It is seen at Wallington Ponds, near Sutton, in May 1986 on a London Regional Transport route.

you see of them is the body, and sometimes the same makes of body get put on different chassis. But they're different underneath, of course.'

'What's so important about a Dennis, then?'

Deep breath. 'The single most important thing about a Dennis is that it is not a Leyland.'

Touché.

'I don't see how you tell one bus from another'

You mean you can't tell a Northern Counties-bodied double-decker from a Park Royal? You mean the very Metro-Cammell Weymann-ness of a Metrobus does not assail your senses?

All right; well I can not tell a Toyota car from a Mazda. But I am quite prepared to accept that there are differences. With buses it is the same thing, really.

Different in what way? Well bear with me for a moment. You see that double-decker over there? Look above the upstairs front window. That ventilation grille is very characteristic of Northern Counties. See? That one by Park Royal is quite different, and look at that Metrobus — an asymmetric windscreen. Two halves of different depths.

No, that's not all there is to it. In fact it's like putting the cart before the horse really. You notice overall differences first. Then maybe you try to pin them down, and you pick up the details.

Why do I look for overall differences? I don't, really. They just seem to demand attention. I mean they are self-evident.

Yes, I know a bus is a bus. I know it doesn't matter what shape or colour it is as long as it comes when you want it. I have cursed buses as much as you have when they have not been the one I wanted. But that does not make them any more or less interesting. I mean, you probably know what a Rolls-Royce looks like. You may even admire them. That doesn't mean you are planning to own one, or even go for a ride in one.

I'll tell you what; how would you like to know how to distinguish a MCW-bodied DMS Fleetline from a Park Royal version? At 100 paces, that is. You wouldn't?

'I recognise the ones with the entrance at the back'

Down two flights of worn stone steps and I'm about to emerge from the tenement, a deceptively forbidding access to a cheerful Glasgow dwelling.

A bus is pulling away just out of my view. Nothing unusual, until suddenly it strikes me that it's a Routemaster. No mistaking that muted roar. I step into the sunshine to see one of London's open-platform veterans rounding the corner. It looks slightly odd in Kelvin's racy blue and yellow livery, yet also

Above:
The chassis of this Dominator in the fleet of local authority Hyndburn Borough Transport, Accrington, was built by Dennis. This authority previously bought Leylands with similar East Lancs bodies before switching allegiance. It is seen in May 1985.

Above right:
Not much of an advertisement for its (virtually anonymous) operator, and arguably not even an effective advert for its Vauxhall-Opel sponsor, this Alexander-bodied Scania is one of only two bought for trials by the Tyne & Wear PTE. It is seen in May 1985.

Right:
The top ventilator is the most obvious point of divergence between the Northern Counties body on the left and the Park Royal one beside it. In fact the Northern Counties front end is altogether squarer, although paradoxically it has a curved windscreen whereas the other is flat. They were photographed in Oldham in August 1985.

extraordinarily familiar. And that sound — a piece of quintessential London atmosphere, miraculously transplanted.

'They've dug out some real old ones', some friends told me the night before. 'They must have had them stored away somewhere.'

'Those will be the buses they've bought from London', I suggested. No sense in calling them Routemasters, they are simply 'old-type buses'.

Amused dissent. The SMT (or whoever they are now) might have some funny ideas, but not *that* funny.

'Truly. It's to get people on and off faster. They always have conductors, you see. Besides, they're cheap to buy.'

'So we're getting stuck with London's cast-offs, are we?'

Well, Londoners might not see it that way. After taking Routemasters for granted for 30 years, they've got a bit more protective about them now. The name has even been bandied around in the press. Londoners have finally cottoned on to the fact that such buses have benefits in speed and boarding times, and are no longer found elsewhere. Or they weren't until London Buses started selling them off. The only thing is, people now tend to use the term Routemaster as though it meant any old-type bus. How do you explain that Routemaster is a model name? How do you tell them it was unique even in its own day — the most advanced of its kind?

'They seem a bit noisy. And they've got no doors.'

'I like the ones with advertisements all over'

Well, I don't. In fact I've have got a positive blind spot about them. My camera shies away whenever one comes into view.

The problem with all-over advertisements is their utter irrelevance to everything that is interesting about buses. For a start, there is no livery in view, and livery is Extremely Interesting. In fact uniformity, and variation within it, really lies at the heart of the matter. Part of the mystique of a bus is knowing there are others that look more-or-less the same. Plus others again that look quite different, but also look like each other. More or less.

Are you following this so far? Anyway, all-over advertisements rule out all that interest. Not only do buses in them not look like each other, but sometimes they hardly look like buses at all. It's not that anyone wants to go round counting the number of rivet-heads. Do they? But how can you get a proper impression of the vehicle if you can hardly see it?

Besides, liveries become linked with the places where you see them. That is one reason why National Bus red and National Bus green were such a disaster — they robbed bus fleets of local character. All-over adverts do the same.

They do help bus companies pay the rent, though. And, just occasionally, they can look quite nice. How about British Telecom's blue and yellow scheme? Not too bad, maybe — if you could have a whole fleet of it, and not just one bus at a time.

And what if an operator has just a couple of examples of a particular bus model and the only one to appear is carrying an all-over advertisement? You clench your teeth and take the picture, that's what.

'I suppose you go to all the rallies?'

There's one place where outsiders have no need to pour scorn on enthusiasts. They manage quite happily to bring it upon themselves. 'Would you mind moving out of the way please?' A bevy of photographers glare impatiently at you. Photographing this Bristol SC4LK is a toil to be endured — that is the clear message in their look. Gradually you acquire a haunted feeling, and by the time you leave you are frozen into near-immobility.

I sometimes take pictures at rallies myself, but I'm never quite sure why. Do I want a record of every extinct livery that has been recreated? Do I want a picture of every single preserved RT? It's hard to be conscientious about it, somehow — and even harder to take the pictures without offending someone.

At least the enthusiasts tend to acknowledge each other's presence, and stay out of the way. Not so the public, who always seem to stroll into view at the instant you're going to take the picture.

In a way you can't blame them when there is an intriguing-looking but microscopic account of the bus's history stuck inside the windscreen, and even when they have finshed pouring over the badges and trophies from previous events, the placard bearing them still leans on the radiator, obscuring the view.

The people whose buses they are usually seem genial enough. But they do tend to have a kind of other-worldliness about them as they sit discussing gearboxes and sipping tea. They may be showing their labour to the world, but they seem to view it with a jaundiced eye.

Above:
A fleet of buses in this well proportioned British Telecom all-over advertising livery might have looked quite effective, although on their own such liveries can seem irrelevant to the operator's image. This Devon General Bristol VRT with ECW body is seen in Exeter in September 1984.

Rallies can be fun, and they're a place where the public and enthusiasts can meet. But imagine going to one every other week.

'Have you been to the bus museum yet?'

After initial bemusement, a look of comprehension sometimes dawns. Of course, it says, there must be some kind of academic interest here. So, 'We've got a fascinating bus museum over at Cheetham Hill (or Albert Drive). Have you seen it yet?'

I nod devoutly, if it's either of those two places. Yes I've seen them, and yes they're both splendid. But on their own, they're not really what buses are about. If they were, it would be rather a meagre interest.

The real interest is generated by the ordinary, everyday buses out there in the street. Plus, perhaps, the ones that used to be there in the past. The museums do a marvellous job of preserving some of those, but you can't really appreciate them unless you can also appreciate the ones running now.

'The ones in the street?' Mingled disdain and embarrassment. Then an effort to rally. 'So you're a kind of social historian?'

Am I? It certainly sounds impressive. Does it mean studying changing fashions? There's been enough of that lately, with deregulation and minibuses and fleets of big buses dwindling. Does it mean capturing the urban landscape as well as the buses in it?

All right. I give in. I'm a social historian, but I don't need to go to the museum to prove it.

'We get four buses an hour now'

Some people, I have discovered, actually know about buses. Ordinary people, that is; people with no avowed interest in the subject. They tell me earnestly that the route near their house has a more frequent service now than it did six months ago. But the company is still running Nationals on it, not minibuses.

This alarms me. Not the information, that is, but the fact that it has been conveyed to me. What am I supposed to say about it? I nod and try to look impressed so they tell me again. Obviously I'm failing in some crucial way to give the correct response.

Maybe I should be explaining how this change reflects the company's policy. But I'm not sure that I know what its policy is. Or perhaps I should enthuse about the con-

Above:
Even non-enthusiasts usually manage to distinguish front-engined, rear-entrance buses from the rest. This former London Transport Routemaster of Clydeside Scottish looked smart and businesslike when photographed in Paisley in August 1986.

venience of the improved service. I try enthusing, but it doesn't quite work.

People like this who know about buses tend to be people who are enthusiasts of something else. Trains, maybe. Or boating holidays. They seem certain that my interest must parallel theirs. Maybe I act the same way towards them. The worrying thing is, sometimes they turn out to be bus enthusiasts. They know all about routes and timetables and headways and layovers. And they tell me with a deep sense of wonder how this United Counties route used to run *all the way through to Aylesbury*.

Usually, people just want to share in what must seem a rather obscure interest — and maybe to show that they actually know something about it that I don't. But their brisk practicality sometimes arouses misgivings.

'I took these pictures for you'

Sunrise on a rain-drenched street in Moscow. Grey clouds above, but brightness breaking through near the horizon, and the hint of a rainbow. There are few pedestrians about on the broad expanse of concrete, but some crowded yellow buses are shuttling people to work, and a red and white Ikarus coach waits.

I've never seen this landscape myself; if I had, I don't suppose this is precisely the picture I'd have taken. Too much empty space; too many trolleybus poles. But the point is, someone took it for me; and without being asked. This gives it a quality all its own. It says 'I may not see the fascination, but I acknowledge it'. It says someone thought of you in a distant place.

What do you do with pictures like this? A six-wheeler Scania with Nielson coach bodywork in Rio? A Utic AEC in Lisbon? A Leyland Worldmaster in Jerusalem? A Bristol VRT on the Isle of Wight?

Relatives, friends, colleagues — they have all contributed to this collection. Sometimes the picture is slightly out of focus. Sometimes someone stepped in front of the camera. Often only part of the bus is in view. Sometimes I would have been glad to have taken the shot myself.

But I didn't. And in days gone by, I've been tempted to explain this to them. The pleasure of bus photography, I've felt like saying, is taking the picture yourself. Yet this would be

missing the point. Whatever the significance, each picture is a gesture — even the ex-London Fleetline photographed a few streets away, so I keep them with a growing sense of gratitude. Maybe they will prompt me to visit more of these places and come back with my own definitive views. But the spirit of the originals is unassailable.

'In all honesty, what do you get out of it?'
Stockport on a late summer afternoon. The sky is clear and it's warmer than it's been for weeks. Workers linger in the sun.

I've come here in pursuit of fleetnames. If GM Buses is going to have 16 of them for different areas, I've decided that I'll have a go at photographing them all, yet I don't want this to turn into a great marathon that keeps drawing me back. So I'm trying to slot in as many as possible today. I covered central Manchester between jobs this morning, and I should have time to go on to Ashton after this. Then maybe Oldham? See how the light holds.

But the post rush-hour calm is seductive. People stroll, chat, plan their weekends. Even buses leaving the big open-air bus station seem unhurried. I feel an impulse to abandon the pursuit and to merge into this placid scene.

I plan a picture and idly scan round for the unexpected. No ex-North Western VRs and REs now, anyway; no open-platform Titans, ex-Stockport Corporation. Just Atlanteans, Fleetlines, Metrobuses, Olympians. Not even Mancunians any more.

Suddenly I notice something I had no idea I would be seeing; a Northern Counties double-decker that is subtly different from the rest. Wrong radiator grille — and wrong sound. For a moment the pink Express livery throws me; then I realise it is one of the 30 Northern Counties-bodied Metrobuses delivered to GM Buses. I had no idea they were in service yet.

Rousing myself, I snatch an impromptu shot of it. Then I follow it from the pedestrian area into the bus station and get a better picture of it there. Just to convince myself of what I've found, I check the letters on the wheel hubs. No disputing it: MCW.

I wander back out through the archway, marvelling. The scenery seems to have more edge to it now, somehow, and the mission more purpose. Casual shots of boring Atlanteans are simply part of the endeavour.

In the car park I hesitate again, savouring the summer air. Traffic rushes past where the M63 is cut into the hillside. The sun is still warm.

Pursuing these fleetnames is silly; I can see that. But just as the Metrobus added piquancy to the day, so the wider pursuit sharpens experience and gives perspective. The pleasure, if you like, is simply to be standing here. No one can challenge that, and it defies any further explanation.

Maybe next time I come here, minibuses will have over-run the place. Maybe quite recent Atlanteans will have been sold through deregulation cuts. I head for Oldham, to catch silly fleetnames before sunset.

Far left:
Would-be photographers wait vainly for a clear view in Battersea Park in May 1985 at the annual bus rally linked to the Brighton run.

Left:
Social historians or the next generation's bus enthusiasts? These young artists are seen in the London Transport Museum, Covent Garden, in May 1984. Did anyone mention to them that the buses outside could be just as engrossing?

Below left:
Chassisless coaches built by Portuguese bodybuilder UTIC with AEC mechanical parts were a UK link that survived the political upheaval in Portugal in the early 1970s. Leyland maintained the link after AEC was closed down in 1979.

Below:
This MCW Metrobus, one of the first ever to receive Northern Counties bodywork, is seen in Stockport in September 1986 during its first week of operation.

Secondhand

John Milnes *provides before and after illustrations of vehicles which found new owners in the aftermath of deregulation.*

Below and top right:
Newport Transport built up a large fleet of Metro-Scanias. VDW 438K is seen in service in Newport on a sunny August day in 1986, and in Dewsbury in rather different weather 12 months later, operating a Huddersfield to Leeds service for Ivy Coaches.

Centre right and bottom right:
This dual-door Plaxton-bodied Leyland Leopard, JDK 922P, was an unusual member of the Greater Manchester Transport fleet and had been new in 1975 to Lancashire United Transport. It is seen outside the now-closed Victoria bus station in Salford — a victim of deregulation — in 1985; and two years later in Sheffield in the maroon and yellow livery of local operator Richardson.

203
LEEDS
IVY
VDW 438K

LEIGH

RICHARDSON
110
JDK 922P
Legal & General.
WINE GUM

Above and below:
Many vehicles changed hands between major operators in 1986 and 1987, and among those affected were Ribble and Southdown. Ribble National CBV 780S was photographed in Blackburn in February 1985 on the Hyndburn Circular service and in Portsmouth, now in Southdown ownership but still painted red, in November 1986.

Right and bottom right:
Greater Manchester Transport withdrew large numbers of buses in October 1985 and these soon found buyers throughout the country. Leyland Atlantean XJA 518L, photographed in Stockport in August 1985, was running for Gash of Newark two years later. It is an AN68 with bodywork by Park Royal, and is an early example of the Selnec/Greater Manchester standard design.

384
MARPLE
7127
XJA 518L

GO GASH
Welcome Aboard
82
GO GASH
XJA 518L

Forty Years Ago

Roy Marshall *offers a selection of photographs from areas he visited in 1949.*

My interest in buses began in earnest when I started Grammar School in 1940, the journey to which required my travelling across the city using three different services. It was not until the middle of the War that I was able to take my first photographs — for Bill Haynes who supplied the films which were then in short supply. This shortage continued until 1948 when a more plentiful supply coincided with my replacing the family Brownie box camera by a more sophisticated folding type. This proved to be an excellent investment which was quickly put to good use and was used the following year when I spent my first holiday away from my family or my father's relations who lived in Elland, near Halifax. This was at Cardiff, since I was limited to my annual holiday entitlement of one week. Otherwise photography had to be restricted to trips out on Sundays or the three Bank Holidays between Easter and August, although an unfortunate plus was a weekly visit to Peterborough for health treatment.

BIRMINGHAM 1647

Seen at Garrett's Green Lane terminus on August Bank Holiday Monday was this new Crossley, one of the first 10 in the Birmingham City Transport fleet. Note the wheel trims which experienced brief popularity.

BURY 132 *(Above)*

One of four Roe-bodied Leyland PSls owned by Bury Corporation seen in Kay Gardens while working the Rawtenstall service on a quiet Sunday in August. It was to be only a few years later that vehicles of this type and size were converted to one-man operation.

HALIFAX JOC 249 *(Below)*

One of the first 8ft wide buses in the Halifax fleet was this timber-framed Park Royal-bodied AEC Regent. The slender pillars were against the advice of the coachbuilder in view of the uncertainty surrounding the durability of relatively unseasoned timber. The terminus is a town centre side street, again popular in Halifax for a period since deregulation prior to the opening of a new bus station.

NOTTINGHAM 782 *(Top)*

Increased demand for services, coupled with extended delivery periods, resulted in Nottingham City Transport purchasing a total of 19 secondhand double-deckers in the early postwar period, including this Brush-bodied AEC Regent from West Bridgford. Next to it is one of 45 Craven-bodied Regents of 1937, the bodies of which gave structural problems resulting in them all being rebuilt over a period at this time.

PONTYPRIDD UDC 29 *(Above)*

Standardisation on Bristols for its heavyweight requirements was the order of the day at Pontypridd UDC until the war intervened to end the practice. This was one of three K5G models delivered in 1939. In the background is an ECW-bodied Regent of Western Welsh.

BARTON 450 *(Top)*

During 1946 and 1947 Bartons were another operator who augmented their fleet — this time with 18 secondhand Titan TD1 and TD2 models. This TD2 came from Leeds and its teak framed Roe body gave such good service that Bartons continued to specify this expensive timber for all new coaches over a period of many years.

BULLOCK & SONS 219 *(Above)*

A Leyland-bodied Titan TD5 in the maroon, red and cream livery of Bullock & Sons is seen at the North Bridge terminus, Doncaster, prior to the merger between this operator and West Riding. New in 1938, it was one of 12 new vehicles bought that year, comprising four chassis models from three manufacturers and fitted with bodies from five different builders.

MIDLAND RED 3140 *(Above)*
A cold day in February sets the scene for this Brush-bodied AEC Regent, one of 50 built for Midland Red. These were the first postwar double-deckers for this operator.

NOTTS & DERBY 320 *(Below)*
In 1933 Notts & Derby converted the lengthy Nottingham to Ripley tram service to trolleybus operation using 15 of these Metropolitan Cammell-bodied AEC 661T models. These vehicles had the English Electric equipment housed behind a dummy radiator. This bus is seen at the Heanor Market Place terminus awaiting departure for Ilkeston in January. These buses worked this service extensively in their later years. Trolleywheels continued to be used almost exclusively by the company at the time rather than the more common sliding heads, due to the short life of the carbon inserts on frosty days.

BOYER OF ROTHLEY *(Below)*

This Strachan-bodied Dennis Lancet utility bus is seen on spare land adjoining St Margaret's bus station, Leicester. It was intended for the Barton fleet but was diverted to Boyer of Rothley, the old-established pioneer operator on the Leicester to Loughborough main road service, then worked by five operators.

GASH OF NEWARK *(Bottom)*

When Gash of Newark introduced their postwar direct service between Newark and Nottingham to take the load off the village services they were so overwhelmed by passengers, including many Royal Air Force personnel from RAF stations en route, that an hourly service was quickly augmented to half-hourly on Saturdays, each departure requiring two double-deckers — eight in all. This view depicts a fairly new Strachan-bodied Daimler CVD6 followed by an ex-Wigan Titan TD1 at Huntingdon Street bus station, Nottingham.

What Might Have Been

Many bus designs get no further than the drawing board. **Basil Hancock** *examines some projects for which the draughtsmen at Eastern Coach Works produced drawings, but which were never built.*

Above:
ECW Drawing No 3889 of October 1947 depicts a 35-seat body on a Leyland Tiger PS1 chassis for Lisbon.

I suppose that we all dream at some time about what might have been, and bus enthusiasts are certainly no exception. Perhaps we imagine our favourite type of bus in the livery of our local operator. Maybe we invent our own fleets or operators of buses, or we may even propose new route networks. Although there have been many different types and makes of body and chassis and a wonderful range of combinations, there are many permutations, layouts and styles which for one reason or another never saw the light of day. But suppose that we could look at some of those vehicles that might have been.

Each manufacturer used to prepare General Arrangement drawings of their products, and often a layout would be made of a vehicle which was never destined to roll out of the factory gates. Perhaps the layout was shown to be impractical or the resulting vehicle would be too expensive to build, but more often than not the drawing was the result of an enquiry from a potential customer who subsequently placed their business elsewhere. A recent opportunity to look through the General Arrangement drawings and index of the much-lamented Eastern Coach Works of Lowestoft revealed a number of such abortive projects, and this article describes and illustrates a few of them. Space does not allow even a mention of most of them, but I have picked out a few of the more choice examples from the period after the end of World War 2.

Inevitably much of ECW's history is bound up with that of Bristol Commercial Vehicles,

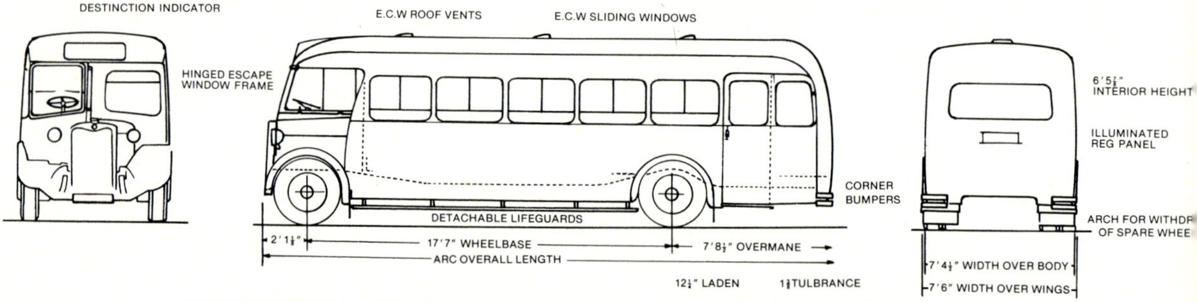

ARRANGEMENT OF 35 SEATER SINGLE DECK BODY ON CROSSLEY S.D. BUS CHASSIS

Above:
This July 1950 design shows a proposed 20-seat body on a Leyland Cub chassis for London Transport.

and many of these proposals also involve chassis designs that similarly never saw the light of day.

As might be expected, much of ECW's early postwar period was spent in restocking fleets ravaged by years of neglect and suffering from the postwar boom in traffic. Most of their output was naturally based on Bristol chassis for the Tilling Group and others, but exports were not forgotten and we soon find that Egypt attracted the attention of the salesmen with a 1946 proposal for a virtually standard rear-entrance single-deck body mounted on a Crossley SD42 series chassis. This was followed up with designs for Lisbon, including drawing No 3889 which shows a fascinating single-deck body to left-hand-drive layout (ie the door on the opposite side) mounted on a right-hand-drive Leyland Tiger PS1 chassis. This was similar to the large fleet of AEC single-deckers and double-deckers which were later supplied to Portugal, though not, as it turned out, with ECW bodies.

By 1950 the ECW draughtsmen were turning their attention to the new underfloor-engined chassisless Bristol single-decker, later to be known as the LS, and among the various designs was a curious rear-entrance coach, similar to (or which maybe even inspired) the Willowbrook-bodied Leyland Tiger Cubs later built for East Yorkshire. However, the most interesting project of that year was undoubtedly the proposal to rebody some prewar Leyland Cubs for London Transport, and three designs materialised. The first drawing showed a 20-seat body with a sliding door, and the second a modified version with improved styling and a glider door. These two envisaged retaining the original Cub wings and bonnet, but the third proposal was far more radical and included an entire new front end of very American appearance, together with a more modern body design. The genesis of the Guy-based GS of 1954 is very apparent from this drawing, No 3961.

By 1954 the potential of the nationalised connection with British Railways was being investigated, with proposals for six-ton platform bodies and box van bodies mounted on Dennis Centaur chassis, but the two most unusual bus proposals of this year involved the Bristol Lodekka. One was for a 58-seat version for the Sheffield Joint Omnibus Committee and the other was for a full-fronted lightweight version, presumably with coaching duties in mind, for an unspecified enquiry. This design, drawing No 4110, indicates that a standard 27ft-long LD-series Lodekka was to be modified by simply adding a nearside windscreen and side window, and a handsome machine it would have been too, though the access to the engine would obviously have been severely restricted. A separate window and nearside cab door would undoubtedly have been more practical.

The existence of Joint Committees (where British Railways had a financial stake in some operations) in Halifax, Huddersfield, Sheffield and Todmorden meant that ECW was eligible as a supplier despite being otherwise barred from markets outside London Transport and the Tilling and Scottish Bus Groups. This was the reason why the Lodekka could be tendered for the Sheffield Joint fleet, and why ECW bodies on Titan and Leopard chassis did eventually enter the fleet. The Lodekka was also tendered for the Sheffield fleet again in 1958, in 55-seat and 59-seat layouts, but before this two attempts were made to interest the Huddersfield JOC in 1956. These were a lowbridge body on an unspecified chassis and a highbridge body on a Bristol KSW chassis, but neither was to be.

The next unusual offering to appear on the scene was a proposal for Crosville in 1958 for a 35-seat Bristol SC4LK body with a detachable top, presumably for seaside duties. Sadly the drawing itself has disappeared, so it is not clear whether the split was to be at waist level or whether fixed side windows were employed with merely a removable roof.

After this things seem to have gone quiet for a few years, but in 1961 the first ideas for rear-engined single-deck chassis were obviously coming out from Bristol, and a whole range of bodies to the new 36ft overall length appeared on the ECW drawing boards, with a mixture of front and centre or rear doorways. Obviously the decision had not been taken to proceed with what became the Bristol RE chassis at this stage because ECW kept their options covered by proposing an alternative mid-engined layout as well, and even the rear-engined layout was covered by a variety of chassis frames and engine arrangements. A typical proposal is to be seen in layout No 4598 which shows a 50-seat two-door bus, notable for the narrow rear exit which bears a remarkable resemblance to that of the standard half-cab postwar body.

Soon after this the RE came on to the scene, and its success inspired a number of proposals for a rear-engined double-deck chassis from Bristol. As is well known, the first such chassis, the Bristol VRL, appeared in 1966 with its engine mounted longitudinally behind the offside rear wheels. What is probably not so well known is that it was originally known as the Bristol N-type and that ECW had worked out a range of single and double-deck bodies for it by 1964. The earlier ones were double-deckers combining a front entrance and staircase with a second staircase leading down over the engine to a rear exit behind the back axle. Other designs had more conventional single door or front-entrance/centre-exit layouts as alternatives. In order to enable standardisation of chassis,

Above:
This illustration shows what ECW drawings 4110 and 4884 might have looked like in practice. On the right is a 58-seat full front body on a Bristol Lodekka LD-series chassis designed in 1954, while on the left is a January 1966-designed 69-seat rear entrance body on a Bristol Lodekka LDL-series chassis.

and to comply with the current trend to low floor single-deckers, a similar range of single-deck bodies was worked out, again with front/centre or front/rear doors. All shared the low floor of the double-decker and in some cases were as little as 8ft 6in in overall height (what suitable buses they would have been for North Western's Dunham Massey route), while one particular specimen even went as far as having inward facing seats only, for about 16 passengers, with a vast standee area.

However while the N-type was being worked out, a counter-proposal from Bristol envisaged a rear horizontal-engined double decker instead, and drawing No 4816 shows the layout of a 36ft 87-seater, with such unusual features as a nearside staircase (with shades of the Guy Wulfrunian and Tyne & Wear PTE) and a large luggage area over the rear engine where the floor height made the provision of seats impractical, not to mention illegal.

In 1966 both ECW and Bristol were freed from the restrictions on their markets and ECW bodies once more became available to the whole of the operating industry, either in combination with Bristol chassis or now on other chassis. A whole range of ideas began to flood out of Lowestoft in response to enquiries, including coach bodies on Albion Vikings, Leyland Leopards and Royal Tiger Worldmasters, single-deck bus bodies on AEC Reliances and Leyland Clydesdales for export, and on Daimler Roadliner chassis for PMT in England. Double-deckers were not forgotten either, with bodies on Leyland

Atlanteans and Daimler Fleetlines for all manner of customers and, more unusually, a design for a 64-seat double-deck body on Leyland Titan PD2A/27 chassis for, not surprisingly, Lowestoft Corporation in 1966. This was followed by a similar 70-seat body on the longer PD3A/2 chassis for Bradford Corporation in the same year.

The standard Bristol-ECW range was not neglected either, and designs for bodies on VRT and RE chassis were proposed for many new customers, of which the most unusual were probably two layouts on RESL and RELL chassis for Kuwait in 1967. The Lodekka chassis was redesigned as a cheaper full-height design for general sale, and although none of the new LDL model (not to be confused with the LDL flat-floor prototypes of nearly a decade earlier) was ever built, layouts for both front and rear-entrance bodies were produced. Drawing No 4884, produced in early 1966, shows a typical rear-entrance 69-seater with a basically standard Lodekka body raised by about eight inches and with correspondingly lower internal wheel arches, though there was now a step from the platform into the lower saloon. Somehow the design seems to lack the elegance and proportions of the standard Lodekka.

The 1970s saw no let up in the pace of new proposals, of which the most interesting included the redesign of the VRT with a four-bay body which was soon superseded by other designs using Leyland Titan (B15) parts, before eventually both ideas were in turn replaced by the Olympian. Export proposals included both single and double-deck bodies on Leyland Atlantean and Olympian chassis in 1978 (fully air-conditioned as well!) for New York, and 110-seat double-deck bodies on Daimler Fleetline chassis for Hong Kong at around the same time.

Perhaps the most unusual layouts produced at this time were a number of proposals for bodying the Leyland-DAB articulated bus chassis produced in Denmark (though in the end the bodies were to be built at Workington and Charles Roe using Leyland National components). The designs involved various door layouts and positions, and drawing No 5259 of 1978 shows a typical proposal, with 67 seats, 42 standees and four sets of double doors.

Even in its final years ECW was investigating new ideas, and three new types of chassis appeared under proposals for their bodywork during the 1980s. At least five layouts were made for ECW-bodied Volvo Citybuses for three different customers, followed soon by other similar designs based on the Leyland Lion underfloor-engined chassis, and a very neat 28-seat body was drawn up for the Dennis Domino to the requirements of a PTE, but sadly, along with all the other designs mentioned in this article, they were not to be.

We can only dream about what might have been.

Below:
An August 1964 design for an 87-seat 36ft lowheight body on a Bristol rear underfloor engined chassis.

Citybus Collection

The Volvo Citybus can be seen with a wide variety of bodywork. **David Barrow** *presents a photographic survey of them at work.*

Underfloor-engined double-deck buses have always been a rare breed in the UK, with manufacturers sticking to the more acceptable engine position of front or, in latter years, at the rear.

However, in 1982 Volvo Bus (GB) introduced an underfloor, mid-engined chassis, called Citybus, suitable for both single or double-deck applications, although considerably more of the latter have been built.

Although Volvo are a Swedish company, the chassis was manufactured and assembled at its Irvine plant in Scotland, using many British-made components. When fitted with a UK-manufactured body, the Volvo Citybus was over 70% British built.

In 1987 all that changed, and the chassis are now no longer built in Scotland but at Volvo's bus plant at Boras in Southern Sweden. The Citybus name was dropped, and the chassis is designated now as D10M. It also lost its perimeter frame, and is now virtually a modified B10M coach chassis.

Far left:
Derby had until recently the second largest Citybus fleet in Britain. A 1983 East Lancs-bodied bus is seen in the city centre on a wet November evening in 1984.

Top:
Derby has three makes of bodywork on its Volvo Citybuses — Marshall, East Lancs and Northern Counties. One of the Northern Counties examples delivered in February 1986 is seen in Derby when new.

Above left:
Nottingham's Volvos all have that operator's familiar and unusual style of bodywork. An East Lancs-bodied version is seen loading in Trinity Square.

Left:
Seven Northern Counties-bodied Citybuses were delivered to Nottingham in December 1985 and January 1986. This one was photographed in Parliament Street depot when only a few weeks old.

Top:
GM Buses have three Northern Counties-bodied Citybuses bought for evaluation. They are based at GM's Wigan depot. This one is seen at the Ribble Enthusiasts Club Rally in 1986.

Above right:
One of Badgerline's Volvo double-deckers is seen returning to Alexander's Falkirk factory in May 1987 after completing a road test prior to delivery. It is fitted with coach seats.

Right:
Photographed outside Walter Alexander's factory is one of Eastern Scottish's 1987 D10Ms with R-type bodywork.
Alexander

Stateside Snapshot

Gavin Booth *describes the volatile American bus and coach market.*

The man on the information desk at New York's Pennsylvania station shook his head and smiled. 'No', he said, 'you won't find these double-deck buses on the streets. They're outta service — they're English.'

I had asked him if he knew where New York's Leyland Atlanteans were. I had spent a few days in Manhattan on my first visit to the United States early in 1979 and had seen nothing of them. I knew eight of them had been delivered in 1976 because I had seen them at Leyland and had driven one on the test-track there. But where in sub-zero New York were they?

My quest for the Atlanteans was prompted not only by chauvinism, but also by a desire to see something *different*. New York, and Boston a few days before, had confirmed what I had always suspected: that all American buses were efficiently but depressingly standardised. There seemed to be perhaps half-a-dozen types of bus and coach — GMC and Flxible (sic) transit buses, Eagle and MCI long-distance coaches, GMC parlour coaches and school buses. Now it wasn't quite as bad as that — there were variants of these types — but variety there wasn't.

Today the situation is rather different. Like Leyland in Britain in the 1970s, General Motors Corporation (GMC) had moved into a position of virtual monopoly and the market was ripe for competition both from US manufacturers and from European exporters. This has happened in the 1980s and the

Below:
Times Square, New York, and a GMC 'new-look' vehicle typical of the transit buses still to be seen in most American cities. Piccadilly Circus has little to fear from New York's equivalent.

Top:
Downtown Los Angeles, and a Flxible 'new-look' of the mid-1970s, showing the lantern-style windscreen. It was in the service of the principal local operator, Southern California Rapid Transit District.

Above right:
AM General's squarer-profiled 'new-look' model, the Metropolitan, seen in service in St Louis.

Right:
New York has a large and growing fleet of the GMC RTS model, all with electronic front destination screens. With over 14,000 examples in service, this has become the most familiar transit model in the US today.

Far right:
One of New York's ill-fated Grumman Flxible 870s, showing the square lines and the extra-long wheelbase of the 40ft bus. New York's Grummans were all withdrawn and sold after a very short life.

repercussions will be felt for many years. From a purely selfish viewpoint, it has greatly increased the bus interest — not that this should ever be the sole reason for visiting this amazing country; but it helps.

Bus enthusiasts are relatively thin on the ground in the US, and information on the buses there is not so easy to find. There are industry magazines like Bill Luke's *Bus Ride*, and *National Bus Trader*, and the British-based *Buses Worldwide* fills in more of the detail, based on members' observations. From these sources, and from four visits to the US, I have pieced together this snapshot of the buses that can be seen and who manufactures them.

For many years the giant GMC, a division of General Motors based in Pontiac, Michigan, dominated the American scene. GMC's bus business was based on the famous Yellow Coach company, bought by GM in 1925. After World War 2, bus production resumed under the GMC Truck & Coach Division. GMC had a virtual monopoly of US bus manufacturing by the mid-1950s, with a range of transit buses (city buses) and inter-city coaches. Only Flxible offered alternative products, but they were always overshadowed by GMC.

GMC's hold on the inter-city market was broken when the famous Greyhound organisation, always big GMC users, bought into the Canadian Motor Coach Industries (MCI) company. Greyhound had become MCI's main customer by 1967, and as the range was available to all operators MCI rapidly became the inter-city market leader, a position the company still holds.

Confusingly, MCI coaches are built in three plants. The company had started in Winnipeg in 1932, and in 1948 Greyhound Lines of Canada, MCI's major customer, acquired a majority shareholding. A decade later MCI had become wholly owned by Greyhound and in 1962 a plant was established in the US to increase capacity as the company widened its markets. Greyhound switched increasingly to its own in-house products and by 1966 GMC found itself squeezed out of this lucrative business. The new plant was in Pembina, North Dakota, and in 1974 a third plant was opened, this time under the Transport Manufacturing Corporation (TMC) name, in Roswell, New Mexico. TMC assembled MCI coaches, principally for Greyhound and its affiliates.

Without the Greyhound business, GMC concentrated on transit buses with its range of 'new-look' models dominating the market from 1959 to 1977. GMC's transit buses had evolved from models built by Yellow Coach in the late 1930s, when US manufacturers had pioneered the concept of rear-engined integrally-constructed transit buses. Between 1939 and 1959 GMC built tens of thousands of 'old-look' transits for US operators. These were small-windowed bulbous looking buses in 35ft or (from 1948) 40ft lengths; most were 7ft 11in wide, though some were 8ft 5in wide. The Detroit Diesel 671 was the standard engine, and transmission could be four-speed synchromesh or two-speed automatic. After World War 2 air suspension became standard.

The long-running GMC 'old looks' were replaced by a new model in 1959. Inevitably, these became known as 'new looks', and can still be seen in large numbers. They were also known as 'fishbowls' because of the distinctive windscreen design with drooping lower corners. The side windows were distinctive

Above:
The most familiar inter-city coach on American roads is the MC-9, which has been in production since 1978. This Greyhound example is outside the United Nations building in New York.

Right:
Loading at the Trailways coach station in St Louis are three Eagle 05 coaches.

Far right:
The Chicago Transit Authority has a number of these MAN artics, a type to be found in several American cities.

too, trapezoid in shape, echoing a fashion that had been started with GMC's classic PD4104 parlour coach in 1953.

The GMC 'new looks' were built over a period of nearly 20 years, from 1959 to 1977, and production continued at GMC's Canadian plant until 1983.

The only real competition for the GMC 'new looks' came from the Flxible and AM General companies. Flxible produced a transit model in Delaware, Ohio, between 1973 and 1978 with a mechanical specification similar to the GMC, and a similar design of side windows to the GMC. The front end is the best point of recognition, as the Flxible sports a Dutch-style lantern windscreen. AM General built transit buses between 1974 and 1978 to a more modern design, with bigger, rectangular side windows, a design shared with the Canadian Flyer model, following from an agreement in 1971.

The fact that GMC, Flxible and AM General all ceased production of their transit models in 1977/78 was not a coincidence. The Urban Mass Transportation Authority had drawn up requirements for the next generation of transit buses, its Transbus designs, which would render previous models obsolete. The Transbus project failed, and the new Advanced Design Buses (ADBs) replaced them, a compromise between traditional and Transbus specifications. The most successful ADB has been the GMC RTS, a most shapely and stylish design that has been in production now for more than 10 years. The RTS quickly took over as the principal transit choice for most operators. In 10 years over 14,000 have been delivered, although the bulk of sales were made in the early 1980s, and falling orders — and perhaps increasing competition — prompted GMC to pull out of bus production in 1987. Fortunately, Greyhound Corporation stepped in to buy the business, acquired the GMC 'tooling pro-

cedures and expertise' and will continue to build the RTS at Roswell under the TMC name.

For much of its life the only competition for the RTS came from the Flxible 870. This impressive-looking vehicle is square where the RTS is rounded, with an amazingly long wheelbase — 24ft 11in in a 40ft bus; the Americans, as you may have gathered, do not believe in metrication. The 870 has not been as successful as Grumman, then owners of Flxible, might have wished. Although it sold in respectable numbers, it was bedevilled with structural problems. New York had bought 851 in 1979 at a cost of $89 million, but by 1983 they had proved so troublesome that the fleet could be seen languishing on a pier in Brooklyn. In 1985 GAC bought 815 for $5,700 each, with the aim of rebuilding and selling them, and New Jersey subsequently bought 120 at $60,000 each. GAC had in the meantime bought Flxible — the ownership of US bus builders has never been simple and straightforward!

An improved version of the Flxible 870 was launched as the Metro, and the 870's reputation does not appear to have harmed it, for transit authorities ordered more than 400 of them in 1987.

The threat to the complacency of the US builders came with the appearance of European manufacturers. One of them, Volvo, did not linger in the US market and pulled out after only 18 months, although a number of articulated buses had been delivered to US operators during that period. The other three have stayed on.

MAN's American model, built in North Carolina, has sold in large numbers to major fleets including Atlanta, Los Angeles, Phoenix, Pittsburgh and Washington. Chicago alone has over 800 in service or on order. Neoplan build the Transliner bus in Colorado, and substantial orders include over 1,000 for Pennsylvania State and over 400 for Los Angeles. The third major European builder is Scania, who export chassis from Sweden and build bodies in Connecticut.

The success of the importers in the transit bus market has not been reflected elsewhere, although several of the European builders have been active in the coach market.

Many of the coaches exported to the US are familiar in Britain — though so far none are actually British. There is the LAG Panoramic, MAN SR range and Van Hool T815, while Neoplan and Setra produce adaptations of normal models and which are designed to meet American requirements more closely. In addition, the Renault FR-1 is sold as the Mack FR-1.

The coach market has been a more difficult nut to crack. MCI/TMC and Eagle have enjoyed the advantage of ready-made markets in Greyhound and Trailways, the two major inter-city operators.

MCI's range has evolved over more than 20 years, with gradual improvements from model to model, and no radical style changes even in the face of European competition. Greyhound has been the principal customer, although MCI models are generally available too.

Greyhound's current model is designated MCI, the successor to MC-prefixed models that culminated in the 1978 MC-9. The MC-9 is still available, but the 1985 MCI family is now the more popular choice. The range is available in two widths, 8ft and 8ft 6in, and as two- or three-axle coaches.

The story of the Eagle range has also been one of gradual evolution; the early examples were built in Europe, but since 1975 Eagle coaches have been built in Texas, many for Trailways and its associates, but also for general sale. Current models in 1987 were the Eagle 10 and the Golden Eagle II.

In 1987 Greyhound's new owners bought out the ailing Trailways business, and with it the Eagle International manufacturing interests. With two excellent models available, it will be interesting to see what buying policies Greyhound chooses to pursue.

Home market competition for the big two came from Prevost, the Canadian manufacturer, with a line in bizarre-looking coaches and an amazing 60ft articulated high-floor coach.

The MCI, Eagle and Prevost models, and some of the imports, have strong similarities. There is no body-on-chassis market as in Britain — a coach is ordered as a complete vehicle, and most feature the same mechanical components. The rear-mounted engine is almost inevitably the Detroit Diesel Allison (DDA) 6V92TA, or one of its close cousins. This V6 unit is fitted to the main transit models — Flxible, RTS, Neoplan — and in the main coach models — Eagle, Prevost, MCI, Van Hool and Setra — with the V8 DDA as an option. Only MAN and Scania fit their own engines, though this does not appear to have deterred buyers.

There are bigger vehicles too. Articulated buses are becoming increasingly common in many cities. Several models have been available. From 1978 AM General imported vehicles in part-finished form from MAN; now MAN build the model in the US. The Hungarian Ikarus artic has also been imported, first by Crown Coach, now by Orion. Volvo came and went with artics; Scania has had a go and even GMC tried an artic based on the RTS design, but this variant was not pursued. Of course there is also Prevost's 60ft articulated coach, with five axles (four in the forward section) and seats for up to 71 passengers. Surprisingly, this was not the first articulated coach model to operate in the US — Continental Trailways bought four from Kässbohrer in the late 1950s.

What about double-deckers? Well, in addition to the New York Atlanteans, Los Angeles received 22 Neoplan Skyliners for express work, but decided in 1986 that they were 'losers' and 'not built for LA'. Which just leaves the Atlanteans, which were sold to Gray Line to operate in San Francisco (initially while the famous cable cars were out of service) and a recent batch of three-axle Olympians for the same operator. The Olympian is available to US operators through a sales agreement with Gillig, the California-based manufacturer.

And in case you are wondering — yes, I *did* find the New York Atlanteans that cold January. The man at Pennsylvania station had been wrong — they *did* run, but only on Saturdays, it seemed, and even that wasn't guaranteed. They were English, after all.

Below:
Neoplan has sold more than 3,000 vehicles in the US, including these Colorado-built Transliner buses, an example of which is seen here in Los Angeles with Southern California RTD.

Above:
Trolleybuses can be found in a few American cities. The Massachusetts Bay Transit Authority runs a batch of these Flyer 800s on services around Cambridge.

Left:
Run to earth at last — a New York Atlantean working a service in January 1979. The eight buses are AN68A.2R models, with Manchester-style Park Royal bodies built at a time when this style had long since been replaced. Leyland did not miss the opportunity to broadcast their parentage with larger than normal LEYLAND lettering.

Sheffield Survey

Yorkshire photographer **Michael Fowler** *illustrates some of the changing vehicles which have operated in and around Sheffield over the last 25 years.*

Above:
In 1964 the BET subsidiary Sheffield United Tours counted this Plaxton-bodied AEC Reliance among its front-line touring coaches. It was photographed in that year on a trip to Holland. The horizontal beading on the body sides was for many years a distinguishing feature of SUT coaches. The SUT name disappeared with the creation of National Travel in the early 1970s.

Right:
The MCW-Leyland Olympic integral was never a common bus in Britain. Sheffield Corporation owned one, a former demonstrator which had been registered in Surrey by the Weymann arm of the MCW organisation. It was new in 1952 and is seen here in 1966.

Above:
The Sheffield operation was in fact run by a joint transport committee — a partnership between British Railways and the Corporation. Among the jointly-owned buses were 32 very late model AEC Regent IIIs which entered service in 1955 with 58-seat Roe bodies and new-look fronts. This was one of the last survivors, photographed in 1973.

Left:
Three Daimler Fleetlines, the first for the fleet, were purchased by the Corporation in 1962. They had Gardner 6LX engines and Weymann bodies. Leyland's Atlantean dominated subsequent 1960s deliveries.

Right:
Among the more unusual Sheffield purchases was a batch of 18 Bristol VRT/SL6G chassis with 73-seat East Lancs bodies delivered in 1972. They joined a fleet in which there were neither Bristol chassis nor East Lancs bodies.

Below right:
Booth & Fisher was one of the many independent operators bought out by the South Yorkshire PTE which took over former municipal bus operation throughout the newly-created metropolitan county from April 1974. Maidstone & District Motor Services was the original owner of this 1961 Weymann-bodied AEC Reliance, photographed in 1975. Booth & Fisher was acquired by the PTE in the following year.

Bottom:
Early deliveries to the newly-created PTE included 62 front-engined Ailsa double-deckers which had striking bodywork built in Ireland by Van Hool-McArdle. They were 75-seaters with two doors and they entered service in 1976-77. No more Ailsas were bought; most subsequent orders went to Dennis or to MCW.

Left:
In 1977 the PTE and Leyland collaborated in trials with the first articulated bus ever to operate in Britain. It was a left-hand drive Leyland-DAB demonstrator and it led to the introduction of limited articulated bus operation in South Yorkshire at the end of the decade.

Below left:
A severe vehicle shortage in 1981 saw the PTE hiring in replacement buses from other operators. These included a Leicester City Transport Leyland Atlantean with Eastern Coach Works body.

Bottom:
A former Portsmouth Corporation Leyland National on the PTE's City Clipper service passes the City Clopper, a horsebus which ran briefly in 1983.

Buses of the Garden Isle

***Michael Dryhurst** has moved home from Surrey to the Isle of Wight. He details what he found when he got there.*

When your local London Transport route, one that you have known and used for over 40 years, passes to London Country so you are no longer served by the bull's-eye roundel, and in turn the local main London Country route goes over to operation by an independent based in the Midlands who uses an assortment of coaches sporting destination details handwritten on a piece of card and wedged into a corner of the windscreen, then it is time to move (the fact that the last of your three children has recently married and left home is coincidental). Although it is not far from Shepperton to the Isle of Wight, metaphorically speaking they are worlds apart.

I have known the island since 1952, when as a 14-year-old schoolboy I had spent a holiday at Lake, between Sandown and Shanklin. At that time I lived in Brighton and so the Tilling flavour of the Southern Vectis fleet was not unfamiliar. The only real difference was that the buses were painted green and most were of lowbridge configuration where there was a sunken gangway on the offside of the upper deck, from which one stepped up to sit on the four-abreast bench seats. But despite the influx of Bristols into the fleet, Southern Vectis boasted a lot of interest at that time, with Dennis Lance I double-deckers with highbridge Eastern Counties (forerunner to Eastern Coach Works) bodies, and single-deckers of that make, Lancets and Aces, plus early Leyland Titans of the TD1 and TD2 variety, all rebodied and sporting the-then updated CovRad radiator.

Despite the fact that at that time the island

Below:
The last day of London Transport operation of the 218 in 1986, and a bemused traveller tries to work out the timetable. What better reason for leaving Shepperton?

Left:
Happy memories of the Garden Isle. This 1931 AEC Regent was photographed running in Shanklin in 1958. It had been bought by Southern Vectis from Brighton Hove & District in the previous year.

Bottom:
Few Tilling companies ran Crossleys. Whitson bodywork was fitted to this coach acquired by Southern Vectis with the business of Nash's Luxury Coaches of Ventnor.

still boasted a comprehensive railway network (all steam, all tank engines) and Southern Vectis services covered the whole island, there were a number of independent stage carriage operators, and I can recall Bartlett's of Shanklin, West Wight Bus Co, Shotters of Shanklin and Seaview Motor Services. The latter company was the most memorable as it operated double-deckers on its route from Ryde to Seaview via Puckpool, two being Leyland PD2 Titans with lowbridge Leyland bodies, delivered in 1950, and one being a prewar ex-Rochdale Corporation AEC Regent with a Cravens body very similar to the AEC trolleybuses operated across the water in Portsmouth. Bartlett's ran a town service in Shanklin with two normal-control Morris Commercial buses with bodies by Wadhams of Portsmouth, a company that has returned to the building of bus bodies in the last few years.

Inevitably, Southern Vectis absorbed many of the smaller coach operators and in the process acquired a mixed collection of vehicles, particularly coaches, all of which helped to preserve the company's image of not fitting snugly into corporate Tilling, and subsequently British Transport Commission, regimentation. Even after World War 2 when standardisation reared its head on a big scale and Southern Vectis purchased standard products from the BTC suppliers Bristol and Eastern Coach Works, the majority of new vehicles bought for the coach fleet were of the Bedford/Duple combination, which again helped to sustain the individual 'feel' of the company, which has prevailed through the NBC era and into privatisation.

A brief look at the current Southern Vectis company and one would be forgiven for thinking that it is highly standardised, but in fact that is not so and there is plenty of vehicle interest. Although the Bristol VRT with standard Eastern Coach Works body comprises the major type in the fleet, with 68 examples covering the period from 1971 to

Right:
In 1987 the oldest coach in the Southern Vectis fleet was a smart 1968 Bristol RESH6G with Duple Commander bodywork — a rare combination 20 years ago and an even rarer one now.

Below right:
This 1971 Bristol VRT, seen climbing out of Ryde, was repainted in Tilling green livery in 1987 and used for the summer season.

Facing page, top:
The privatised Southern Vectis adopted a new livery of marine green and cream as carried by the VR on the right. The bus on the left is still in corporate NBC livery but with the company's own logo having displaced the National double-N alongside the fleetname.

Facing page, bottom:
Southern Vectis operates on contract to Excelsior Holidays of Bournemouth using a Bedford coach in Excelsior's red and cream livery. It has 53-seat Plaxton bodywork.

1981, many of these buses have been painted into the very attractive new livery of marine green and sand which makes them look very different whilst a further 12 (at the time of writing) of the VRT fleet are working across the Solent in Southampton for the company's mainland subsidiary, Solent Blue Line, in a striking two-tone blue and yellow livery. Of the remaining four convertible VRTs that were bought from the erstwhile Hants & Dorset company, two have also been painted into a blue and yellow livery, albeit of different shades and applied in a different scheme, and the other two such buses remain in NBC dual-purpose green and white, although the speed with which the NBC logo was removed from all elements within the company suggests that NBC-style liveries will soon be but a memory on the Isle of Wight.

Currently, there are 17 Leyland Olympian/ Eastern Coach Works vehicles in the fleet, originally numbered 686-702. As this article was being prepared, 701 emerged from the Central Works at Newport as a 64-seat double-decker coach. The vehicle is painted in a striking blue livery and is most impressive, being renumbered into a new coach series as 101. Rumour has it that 702 will be treated similarly which explains, perhaps, why the bus has been given a cherished registration, WDL 142. Delivery of this particular Olympian necessitated the renumbering of the then 702 which became 502, the venerable 1939 Bristol K5G open-topper, still earning its keep in 1987 on the arduous Robin Hill circular.

Question. If Olympian 702 is converted to a coach will it become 102 thus allowing 502 to revert to 702? The answer will probably be known by the time that this is in print.

Over in the West Wight is another old timer

open-topper, this being 501, which is a mere stripling of a Bristol Lodekka LD6G dating from 1956! Both of the two aforementioned buses are in 'Viewfinder' livery — blue and white with turquoise relief. It looks better than it sounds. The company has an open top single-decker, a standard Bristol RELL6G, the Eastern Coach Works body of which has been 'lopped' from the second bay back to the rear, which remains in situ, complete with centre door emergency exit. With the demise of the Leyland National in this fleet, the remaining single-decker buses consist of a handful of the RELL-type Bristol plus five Bristol LHS6L/ECW, two of which came from Devon General. Southern Vectis was in the vanguard of 'minibus mania' and currently has over 20 Ford Transits, all with bodies by Carlyle, painted in a variety of local liveries.

Bedfords still make up a large proportion of the coach fleet, including a number with the Willowbrook Expressway body as built for NBC, and the recent takeover of the West Wight Bus Co has seen full-size Fords come into service. Within the Southern Vectis coach fleet are a number of vehicles of note, particularly 301, the unique Bristol RESH6G with Duple (Northern) coachwork. This entered service in 1968 and is immaculate in its Tilling cream and green livery, whilst the only other remaining Bristol coach is 302, which is an RELH6G dating from 1972 with coachwork by ECW. 309 is the only example on the island of the Eastern Coach Works B51 body, the coach being a Leyland Leopard. At present the coaches carry a number of liveries — National Holidays, National Express, Wightrider (white, orange, green), Fountain Coaches of Cowes (steel blue) and contract liveries such as Excelsior European Motorways of Bournemouth.

During the summer of 1987 the company

RYDE SANDOWN
REDLYNX
RYDE-SANDOWN
APT 876L

AWF 548T

Gateway Foodmarkets
SCHOOL BUS
OSF 134P

Left:
Seaview Services took advantage of deregulation to extend its operations and adopted the Redlynx name and an appropriate livery for its lengthened Ryde to Sandown route which was later cut back to Nettlestone. This is a Plaxton-bodied Bedford.

Centre left:
Cooke's Coaches of Porchfield won some school contracts from Southern Vectis in 1986 and bought a small fleet of ex-West Midlands Metro-Cammell-bodied Bristol VRTs to cover these. These vehicles were also used on regular services at weekends as shown by this bus at Ryde seen while working a service from Newport.

Bottom left:
As well as using contractors, Isle of Wight County Council runs some of its own school services and its bus fleet includes Duple-bodied Fords in the county colours of blue and yellow. This one is seen in Newport.

operated the regular Cowes to Ryde 1A service with a selection of vintage Bristol double-deckers, all of which had at some time been in the Southern Vectis fleet. The buses were LD and FS Lodekkas, an FLF and a Series 1 flat-fronted VRT. All were painted immaculately into Tilling livery with green bodywork and cream relief with dark green lining out and black wheels. They looked absolutely magnificent and long may the treat of summer 1987 continue, hopefully on a more 'touristy' route such as the 16 from Ryde to Blackgang or the 46 from Sandown to Alum Bay and Yarmouth.

What about the independents? Well, they are still here. Seaview Motor Services operates coaches in the traditional Seaview colours of two-tone green and red, but its Ryde to Seaview stage service is marketed as Redlynx with the vehicles operated thereon painted in an all over red livery. With deregulation this bus service was extended at both ends, from Ryde Esplanade to the Haylands district of the town and from Seaview to Sandown via St Helens and Bembridge, but the latter extension was withdrawn in May 1987 under an agreement made with Southern Vectis, the new eastern terminus now being Nettlestone. Moss-Paul Motor Services of Sandown (a merger of Moss Motor Coaches and Pauls Tours) are operating a Monday to Friday service numbered 11, from Bembridge to Godshill via Sandown and Shanklin, Tuesday-only 12, Bembridge to Carisbrooke Castle via Newport, and Saturday-only 1, Ryde to Bembridge, 2, Ryde-Ventnor-West Wight, 3/3A, East Cowes-Ventnor/Whitecliffe Bay, 4, East Cowes-Bembridge and 5, East Cowes-Whitwell. All of these were summer 1987 operations from May to mid-September and it is not known if they will be repeated, although loadings on the 11 appeared good. Routes 1 to 5 are one-person-operated, whilst 11 and 12 are crew-operated using Bedford/Duple coach LDL 728P or Ford/Plaxton PDL 862H. Bedfords and Fords have been the mainstay of the fleet until very recently, when the Leyland Tiger 245 with Duple 320 coachwork became the company's choice.

With deregulation it seemed as if the most serious competitor to Southern Vectis would be Island Travel, a company set up by the proprietor of Cooke's Coaches of Porchfield, on the northwest of the island. Island Travel purchased some much-travelled (South Wales Transport out of West Midlands PTE) MCW-bodied VRT Bristols from Ensign and had them painted in that company's attractive blue and silver livery for use on a number of schools contracts that the company was awarded by the Isle of Wight County Council at the expense of Southern Vectis. At weekends these buses were used on a series of stage carriage routes centred on Newport and in competition again with SVOC, and it was decided that 'dead mileage' on school-days would be eliminated by the buses working as stage services when returning to base which was fine if you wanted to travel from Ventnor to Newport via Niton at 16.50, which no one seemed to. A number of misfortunes beset the company and by July 1987 it had ceased to operate.

On 27 October 1986, Gange Taxis & Minicoaches of Cowes commenced a stage service in competition with Southern Vectis, from Cowes to Ryde via Newport, numbered G1. Two vehicles are used to maintain the route, both being Mercedes, and fares lower than those of SVOC are charged. Another deregulation opportunist is Kim's Tours of Sandown, who operate a Plaxton-bodied Bedford coach on their route 1, from Sandown to Shanklin station. Two weekdays-only Postbus services are operated from Newport to Brighstone and Newtown.

So, if you fancy a trip abroad without the hassle of check-in, passport control or duty-free, then come on over to the Isle of Wight. There is something to cater for all transport tastes including a standard-gauge preserved steam railway and the oldest electric rolling stock on British Rail, the surviving island line being worked by ex-London Transport Piccadilly Line stock of the early 1930s — in Network SouthEast livery!

Simon Butler

Buses and Churches

If buses, because of their size, often dominate town streets so churches also form a significant feature of the British townscape. **Simon Butler** *illustrates a selection of both.*

Above:
York's famous Minster, construction of which started in the 13th century, forms a backdrop for a 1965 Bristol FS in the York-West Yorkshire fleet in October 1979.

Right:
Chester's St Peter's Church stands at the cross on the site of a former Roman fortress. In the foreground a Crosville Leyland National picks up passengers in this 1980 view.

Top left:
The 16th century bulk of Bath Abbey looms over lesser buildings and a B-series Leyland National in the Bristol Omnibus fleet.

Top right:
The 15th century granite tower of Moretonhampstead Parish Church dominates the roofscape in this 1980 view of a Devon General Bristol LH bound for Exeter.

Above:
The Holy Trinity church in picturesque Richmond is now a museum. Two United Bristol REs with dual-purpose ECW bodies await passengers in August 1982.

Top:
St Thomas Parish Church, built in 1710-12, is one of the major landmarks in the centre of Stockton. In the foreground is a Cleveland Transit Fleetline with rather utilitarian-looking Northern Counties bodywork.

Above left:
The spire of the Church of Christ in Jarrow looms over two yellow-liveried members of the Northern General fleet in July 1982. On the left is one of the uncommon Willowbrook-bodied Bristol VRTs and on the right is a Park Royal-bodied Leyland Atlantean of the type found in a number of NBC fleets.

Above right:
A shabby-looking London Country Leyland National passes the slender spire of the Trinity United Reformed Church in St Albans in 1982.

Numbers

We live in a numerate world. **Robert E. Jowitt** considers the fascination of numbers.

The Animals Went In One By One; One More River To Cross; I'll Sing You Twelve, Oh; Green Grow The Rushes, Oh; Ninety-Nine Men Went To Mow, Went To Mow A Meadow . . .

Whether it be to give you greater thirst for more beer to help the next chorus, or just to pass the time while waiting for the bus, train, ferry, or mother-in-law, a cumulative numerical song or ditty has a certain *je ne sais quoi* which lifts it above even such intoxicating classics as *Ilkla Moor, The Wild Rover*, or *Isn't It Grand, Boys, To Be Bloomin' Well Dead* (to quote the drawing room version).

In truth, ever since man first learned to rub two sticks together, numbers have exercised a fascination.

Certain particular numbers have, for diverse reasons, special significance or notoriety; unlucky 13, the 11th hour of the 11th day of the 11th month of 1918, the 39 Steps; and the Bible abounds with them, even to the extent of including the Book of Numbers.

Many people, however, regard books of numbers as containing lists of numerical import rather than Holy Writ. Some such books are mere boring works, ready reckoners or lists of statistics and, of course, statistics known as 'vital' are sometimes applied to young ladies of the type frequently known as 'hot little numbers'. There are also statistical and numerical lists of locomotives, omnibuses and other vehicles, and to many people these make as lugubrious reading matter as do share indexes to paupers.

Below:
London route 1 in RT days in Oxford Street.

Right:
The registration number on this Basque double-decker (crouching room only upstairs) is quite a fine set of figures to compensate for any lack of route number or fleet number.

Far right:
Vienna 2721 beside an April bonfire on route 60. A route 60/62 board is stuffed behind the point iron.

Nevertheless numbers on vehicles have a special attraction; sometimes simply because it is fun — if childish — to collect numbers, sometimes because the number enhances the machine, sometimes because the machine gives character to an otherwise not noteworthy number, and sometimes because each complements the other. The singularly bizarre LNER locomotive with the notable number 10,000 was a case of this, while the unremarkable number 4472 became famous by being on the *Flying Scotsman*.

Railway engine numbers have always been a delight to 'boys of all ages from nine to 90' (as some fools will put it). Numbers on buses and trams have never achieved quite such popularity, but there is no good reason why this should be the case, especially when you consider that vehicles in the street often boast a much greater numerical display; for example a London bus can muster a registration number, a fleet number, a route number and a running number. Few trains can boast such extravagant numeracy . . .

Vehicles numbered one are always conspicuous, but they are somewhat uncommon, because No 1 tends to be the first vehicle in the fleet and thus is likely to have been scrapped a very long time ago. Even where fleet numbers don't just rise higher and higher but revert to No 1 when the original is broken up, the replacement itself comes in due time to be broken up too. (This seems to apply to No 1s more than to other numbers, but this may be an illusion, simply because No 1 is indeed so notable a number.)

In the 1960s, Paris bus No 1 was a modern (1950s) Berliet, much younger than the still-extant prewar open rear-platform Renaults numbered in the 2,000s, 3,000s and 4,000s. Likewise Vienna tram No 1 was a baby, being imported from Germany in the war when Austria was under Hitler's heel, while trailer cars with numbers such as 1909 probably had 1909 as a date of birth as well.

Which reminds us that the years 1931 and 1932 saw the arrival in Paris of the series of Renault TN4 buses which included numbers 1931 and 1932, and in 1927-29 Milano acquired 500 trams based on the celebrated American Peter Witt type, among them being Nos 1927, 1928 and 1929. As the series was numbered from 1501 upwards it could boast every date in modern history, and I recall particularly seeing 1812 and 1914.

I might have seen Milano No 1, too, which

really was an antique, if I had been in the right place at the right time, but I wasn't.

I can, however, claim acquaintance with other original No 1s such as the Oberrheinische Eisenbahn Gesellschaft inter-urban tram No 1 from the magnificent 1914 steam-replacement set 1-18 (I saw it rushing towards Mannheim on a grey day, and managed to photograph some of its sisters), and the Manx Electric inter-urban car No 1 of 1893 (which anyone visiting the Isle of Man can still see). I have also seen 'single figure' tramcars in Duren, Fribourg and Schaffhausen, and also on the Swansea and Mumbles, and, I may add, single figure trolleybuses in Rotherham, Mexborough and St Etienne; which is to say that where these arrived in batches of one to 10 or so, then seeing No 5, for example, is nearly as good as seeing No 1.

In London you had a chance of seeing more than one No 1 — even if you were unlikely to encounter RT1 and RM1 at once, you might in the course of a day find SM1, MB1, XA1 and DMS1. Then you might find LUC 1, which sounds rather charmingly like 'Lucy' and was the registration number of RT1921. The registration numbers of RTs bore no relation to the fleet numbers, whereas RM1921 acquired the number plate ALD 921B. Green RT3333 was LYR 552, RT4444 was NXP 798, red RT1111 was JXN 139, but RM1111 was registered 111 CLT.

In Paris about this time you could meet Chausson No 1111. Others among my favourite Parisian numbers, apart from No 1 already mentioned, were the Saviem OP5 buses Nos 333, 500, 555, 999, 1000 and 1001. You must learn here that Paris buses do not have registration numbers; they are known by their fleet numbers, and, for further identification when on the road, running numbers which can change from day to day. The Prefect of Paris Police authorises a certain number of vehicles to run on each route, and the 'police' plate attached each day to the bus consists of the route number plus two figures starting from 01 and ascending to the maximum quantity permitted.

These numbers, eg 20-01, also serve for internal timetable purposes. It would be rare, though not impossible, for a police number and a fleet number to match but it has to be remembered that not all route numbers,

which started at 20, were adopted, and that no route would have more than a maximum of 30 or so vehicles. Thus the rather choice Renault 3339 (three threes are nine!) could never have been seen with a 33-39 police plate because there was no route 33, and if there had been it would have had less than 39 buses on it. Likewise Renault 3401 couldn't have sported a 34-01 police plate because there was no route 34. However 3901 could have boasted 39-01, and 4301 be seen with 43-01 if those buses were housed in the depots working 39 and 43.

Lyon and St Etienne trolleybuses have, like Paris buses, fleet numbers instead of registration numbers and, I suppose, some indication in the 'police' vein, though it is not so readily visible as it is in Paris. All other French trolleybuses and buses (not least buses in Lyon and St Etienne) have normal registration plates. Marseilles vehicles' numbers end in 13, the number of the *département* of Bouches-du-Rhone, those of Rouen and Le Havre in 76 for Seine-Maritime. The secondhand trolleybuses in Le Havre had numbers ending in 76 too, not in 67 as they had when in Strasbourg, since when French vehicles change hands they change numbers too. A secondhand Paris bus in Tours has a number plate suffixed 37, and a secondhand Paris bus in Paris carries the Seine 75.

There is a certain logic so far as route numbers in Paris are concerned, in as much as all (or nearly all) of the 20s start from the Gare St Lazare, the 30s from the Gare de l'Est, the 40s from the Gare du Nord, 70s from the Hotel de Ville and 90s from the Gare

Left:
An ex-New York Third Avenue tram on route 331 in Vienna, at a stop for routes 132, 231 and 331. This can cause great confusion unless one is well equipped with a map and dictionary. Trailer 1258 was bang up to date in the early 1960s.

Below left:
Vienna trailer No 1911 was built in 1909, and when new was numbered in the 3100 series and had a clerestory roof.

Below:
A secondhand Paris Saviem OP5/3 in Arles, deprived of Paris route numberbox and fleet number, but consoled by a Bouches-du-Rhone (13) registration plate.

Montparnasse. Geographically, 50s, 60s and 80s are rather more vague, and the system is spoiled where routes are shortened from their original termini. Route 67 starts from the Place Pigalle, famed for having its pavements and cafés ornamented by some of the 'hottest little numbers' in all Paris.

Round the edge of the city is a route called PC for *Petite Ceinture* (Little Belt), where most of the urban routes terminate. Outside this, all the suburban routes are numbered from 100 upwards, in no very apparent order, while the outer ends of some of them are numbered from 200; which is to say, for example, the 150 stops everywhere but the 250 rushes the length of the 150 at great speed and then stops everywhere on the extension beyond the end of the 150.

Vienna trams as I remember them in my youth — amid a wondrous collection of girls with short tight skirts and lacquered back-combed hair, choice numbers again — employed a route numbering system with elements of the Paris suburbs. In the middle of the city some of the circular routes had letters, but the radial routes were numbered anti-clockwise increasing more or less logically from 16 in the northeast round to 78 in the east. Outside, the 60 turned into the 360, the 67 became the 167, the 331 appeared to extend beyond the 31 and the 231 beyond that. Buses with the same numbers as the trams started at outer tram termini and worked out to the wilds of the Vienna Woods and the banks of the Blue Danube; so to go to Inzersdorf you would go part of the way on a 65 tram and the rest on a 65 bus — at least my map told me so, I never discovered if it was true — or by another way on a 66 tram and then a 66A bus. What was the significance of the A?

Vienna also boasted a route 0, but I don't know whether this was 'nought' or 'Oh'.

If 0 was the lowest route number you could find, Neuchatel had a trolleybus line which I suppose was 1 and 2 combined, but the route number appeared to indicate a half.

Two of the King Alfred routes from Winchester, 8 and 9, which forged into the dreaming downland and sleepy trout streams of Hampshire were combined for certain workings and displayed both numbers. Indeed on one occasion I heard two pretty damsels reading this out as 'eight-ninths'.

Among the highest route numbers were those of the London trolleybuses, numbered in the 500s and 600s to make sure that no one would confuse them with the motor buses which were numbered between one and 250 (give or take a few digits). When the trolleybuses were withdrawn their route numbers were withdrawn too, and the replacement buses were given new route numbers in the upper 200s, even where the route remained effectively unchanged. There may very well have been some logic in this somewhere, but I failed to find it, and I must admit that I never understood London route numbers anyhow.

To return to sense we shall return to Hampshire, or a corner of it which the bureaucrats now call Dorset. The town itself is still called Bournemouth. Its trolleybuses had reasonably sensible route numbers. Nearly all services started from the Square (actually a circle with rosebeds and a clock tower and the site of the former town centre tram station) and numbers 20-25 all travelled

up Old Christchurch Road to the Lansdowne, while Nos 26 and upwards into the 30s ascended Richmond Hill to Cemetery Junction. The main exception to the rule was the 34 which reached Cemetery Junction via Old Christchurch Road and the Lansdowne. Beyond the Lansdowne and Cemetery Junction respectively the routes ran basically east and north, not without considerable variations of compass point on their outer extremities, the 32 coming down south-easterly to meet the 20 and 24 at Iford. And 20, 21, 22, 23 and 24 all proceeded from the Lansdowne along Christchurch Road (readers may ask why this wasn't called New Christchurch Road, but I don't know the answer) via Boscombe, to a gloomy place called Pokesdown (supposedly a corruption of Puck's Down, not that there is now any sign of Puck) at which point they divided, some to lose themselves in further reaches of garden-gnomeland, and the 20 and 21 to re-unite in Christchurch, where they turned round on a turntable.

The 25, however, did not do these things. To begin with it started in Westbourne, a long way west of the Square, rather than from the Square itself. Like the 34, it turned away at the Lansdowne up Holdenhurst Road. Unlike the 34 it didn't turn off to Cemetery Junction but kept on along Holdenhurst Road until it turned off at Ashley Road to go down and meet the 20-24 in Boscombe. Trolleybuses on the Holdenhurst Road section of the 25 were regularly graced — in termtime in about 1959 — by a very beautiful girl from the Bournemouth School for Girls which in those days was near the Lansdowne

Left:
Mobilefones are clearly hot little numbers on a much be-numbered preserved Paris Renault TN4H.

Far left:
An example of numerical inconsistency, seen in Southampton. The bus behind the 'No right turn' sign has registration and fleet number 236, while No 147 is registered WOW 537J and 173 is registered PCR 296M. And is there really a route 111 in Southampton, as 173 would have us believe?

Left:
The very last moments of Bournemouth trolleybus route 25 on 12 September 1965. Vehicle 242 turns from Ashley Road to Christchurch Road at the end of its final journey, thus abandoning the 25 to diesel smells and memories.

— though later it was transferred, girl, book, and teacher, as you might say, to new premises near the new trolleybus/bus depot in Castle Lane. Let it be noted that Bournemouth re-housed its transport first and its schoolgirls second. As to this girl who travelled along Holdenhurst Road by trolleybus I called her Miss Route 25, until I was able to discover eventually, by the exercise of great guile and with enormous difficulty, that her name was Judith Silverman. Even this did not further my acquaintance with her and I could do nothing but admire shyly and adore desperately her lovely brown eyes across the smart moquette seats below the butter-dish lamp glasses of a 1950 three-axle BUT.

A curious defect in the Bournemouth route numbering system occurred along Christchurch Road, because trolleybus route 20 shared it with Hants & Dorset route 20. The trolleybuses, as has been mentioned, went to Christchurch, but the Hants & Dorset buses went on to New Milton, Lymington and Southampton. My mother had a friend, a very respectable lady in spite of being known both as Mrs Lear and Mrs Ormerod, who was instructed to catch a 20 from Christchurch Road to New Milton. Seeing a bus numbered 20, and being far too respectable to notice whether it was in Bournemouth yellow or Hants & Dorset green — or indeed to notice anything else about it — Mrs Ormerod flagged it down and demanded of the conductor if it was going to New Milton. 'No, my dear, we haven't got the wires out there yet!' he said, and the trolleybus moved onwards, the conductor hooting with unseemly laughter on the back platform — or so Mrs Lear recounted it.

The trolleybuses, or course, were never intended to go to New Milton which was far beyond the borough boundary and even today is still in Hampshire — just. Mrs Ormerod subsequently spent much time in a variety of mental homes and lunatic asylums and is thought to have died of an overdose in a Brighton boarding house.

By the time that happened the Brighton trolleybuses had already been scrapped, or sold to Bournemouth, and the Bournemouth trolleybuses were scrapped eventually, too.

And me, I had become much more involved with other Bournemouth girls, one from the Roman Catholic school for girls who lived near the un-numbered trolleybus route to the old Southcote Road depot and another, actually ex-Bournemouth School for Girls, who lived near routes 20-24. In these cases, I had no need to describe the girls by route numbers; I had far closer terms of endearment for them.

I never heard what happened to Judith Silverman, except that I believe her home was destroyed by a by-pass. She remains forever just a memory of brown eyes and a number to conjure up marvellous unreachable delights — Miss Route 25. A dull enough number, perhaps, but enchanted!

Now, to conclude these numerical wanderings, I can only add: *The Animals Went In Ten By Ten; One More River To Cross! If You Want Any More You Can Sing It Again! One More River To Cross . . .*

Peak Period

Derbyshire County Council has played an important role in preserving and promoting weekend public transport in the Peak District. **Roger Kaye** *illustrates some of the vehicles and operators serving the area in the mid-1980s.*

Above:
The Mam Tor road from Castleton to Chapel-en-le-Frith has been closed for the last decade but is popular with hikers because of the views which it affords. Trent's service from Ilkeston to Castleton goes part-way along the Mam Tor road on Sundays. A Plaxton-bodied Leopard awaits hikers at the terminus.

Right:
A former PMT Bristol RESL in the Silver Service fleet is seen heading from Biggin village towards Alsop-en-le-Dale in August 1986 on the Peak Pathfinder service.

Left:
Deregulation brought some new operators to the Peak District including Derby City Transport. Here a 1976 AEC Reliance with Plaxton body climbs out of Dovedale on a 1987 Peak Pathfinder journey to Ashbourne.

Below left:
Deregulation also brought Crosville minibuses into the Derbyshire hills. This Freight Rover Sherpa is operating a circular Sunday service which links Macclesfield, Leek, Ashbourne and Buxton.

Bottom:
The Chesterfield to Macclesfield service is operated jointly by Crosville and Trent under contract to Derbyshire County Council. A Crosville Leyland Leopard with Duple Dominant body passes Chatsworth House in June 1987.

Top:
In 1986 a new service was started from Rochdale to Crich Tramway Museum. It was initially operated by Greater Manchester Transport but in 1987 the operation was taken over by Rossendale Transport. Rossendale's Leyland Olympian coach climbs through Chatsworth Park. It has East Lancs bodywork and was new in 1987.

Above right:
The West Yorkshire PTE provided a link between Huddersfield and Crich in 1986, using on this occasion in June an appropriately-liveried Leyland Atlantean with Roe body. The trip takes just over three hours and passes through Holme Moss, Glossop, Buxton and Matlock.

Right:
A Greater Manchester Northern Counties-bodied Leyland Olympian approaches the summit of Snake Pass in 1986 on its way to Glossop.